BUCKEYE

Casey Morales

AUTHORCASEYMORALES.COM

Dedication

To Denise.

A woman who has loved thousands, fostered hundreds, adopted twelve, and bore two.

A woman with a heart that knows no bounds; the heart of a mother.

To Denise, the selfless.

My sister.

PREFACE

As you may have guessed by the Dedication, my family has some experience with the children, the system, and the challenges parents working within foster care face. My oldest sister, Denise, has served the needs of children for more than forty years.

And thus, so has our family.

Some of my earliest memories involve visits to her home, where troubled teens cried or screamed or played. Some snuck out back to smoke, while others embraced the little brother who innocently approached their protective shells.

I met every kind of child, with every skin tone, accent, background, and personality.

I met those who appeared to be fine, and those who wore their struggles openly.

I watched as elation brightened faces on the day they met their "forever parents," and witnessed the vanishing, crestfallen shoulders of those who were shuffled out of my sister's care and on to their next temporary home.

The story you are about to read is not a typical MM romance.

It portrays people from my memory, real children I met and played with, teenagers my sister struggled to help, and others whose smiles brightened the world.

I could never write simple MM romance, where rainbows and unicorns appear around every corner. My writing has to mean something, to *say* something.

Please know two things as you begin.

First, this story is personal. It is a labor of love, written with someone in mind whose *life* has been a labor of the ultimate love and compassion. The characters are modeled after people from our past. I took some liberties to shape parts of the foster system to a book, but most of what you read is what we have seen and experienced personally.

Second, while some scenes portray challenging situations and even more challenging children, the intent of this work is to remain positive and hopeful. There is so much love here. And yes, there is an HEA born of a beautiful love between two men.

Again, to Denise: Thank you for your incomparable heart and tireless work. You have made an incalculable difference in the lives of so many who would have never known a mother's love. I respect and admire you so much. You are my hero.

One

NICK

My brain knew it was just part of the game, but my heart felt like somebody had yanked it out, stomped on it, and tossed it out the window.

I shifted in my seat and adjusted the flimsy airplane pillow in a failed attempt to get comfortable. I'd never been bulky, but at six foot three, the middle seat made my knees feel like they were in my chest. Comfort wasn't really going to happen, so I settled for a position resembling a pretzel and closed my eyes.

Nashville had felt like home.

But my team had sucked—at least, the most vocal members of the team did. Santiago and his brood were always talking crap, throwing not-so-subtle gay slurs in my direction. The coaches rarely said anything, and the other guys, the ones clearly bothered, were too afraid to hurt their own standing on the minor league audition stage to speak up.

And for what? Why all the adolescent abuse?

I'd never brought my personal life into the locker room or onto the field. Hell, I hadn't even dated or been out to a bar since making it onto the roster. A shot at pro baseball was far too big to risk with an overheated libido.

Yet, they rarely missed an opportunity to gin up laughs at my expense.

I told myself it was just locker room talk, that they weren't really serious, and none of it mattered. When we hit the field, we had each other's back. That had never wavered. I carried my weight, racking up a .301 batting average and leading the team in error percentage. In any other dugout, I'd be seen as a leader, not a mark.

Still ...

I shifted again, then moved the pillow from behind my head to behind my back, then tossed it onto the floor near my feet. The team would never pay for a minor leaguer to fly first class, but they'd at least booked a direct flight. I'd only have to play the origami game for an hour and a half, so I gave up on sleep and looked across my row mate out the window at the passing clouds.

My brain buzzed with questions.

What would Ohio be like?

Would Columbus be as cool as Nashville?

Would the team be filled with more players like Santiago, or would I finally get to be just another player?

How long would this be home? Should I even bother trying to settle in?

Every coach I'd ever had offered the same advice after an error or tough play: "Focus on the next play. The past is done. Nothing matters but what's next."

Easy for them to say. They hadn't bobbled the ball, or struck out, or whatever thing a player might do to earn that pearl of wisdom.

It's far harder for a player, especially one in the heat of battle, to heed those words.

But here I was, leaving the crib of my pro ball youth to start the next chapter with a new team. The Clippers had a solid reputation as a collegial team with a respected coaching staff and professional front office. I did a little cyber digging and was pleased to find the team actively giving back to the local community, even supporting some local charities aimed at the rainbow family—*my* family. You'd never see my old management sullying their Bible Belt rep by working with struggling gay kids.

Guess I shouldn't be bitter.

Eyes forward, toward the future, on to the next play.

Blah, blah, blah.

I was still bitter.

At Santi. At his friends who enabled him. At the coaches who tacitly approved, then tossed me aside despite my stellar record on the diamond. At my teammates who didn't stand up, even though I told them not to. At myself for allowing ...

Ding.

"Ladies and gentlemen, that bell indicates our final descent into Columbus. Please stow your tray tables and return your seat backs to their upright and locked position ..."

I rubbed my eyes and checked my watch: Four twenty-one.

I was supposed to be at the field by five. I'd be late on my first day.

"Guess it's good the game doesn't start until seven," I muttered to myself.

"Sir?" The teenager in the aisle seat next to me leaned over.

"Nothing. Sorry. Was just thinking out loud."

She nodded and turned back to her dog-eared paperback, some smutty romance she'd probably read twenty times. I could just make out the man-chest on the cover each time she turned a page. Fabio could indeed have butter, if he ever tired of faking it. With a chest like that, he could have pretty much anything he wanted.

The plane descended smoothly, then thunked to the ground less so. I grabbed my duffel bag from the overhead and race-walked, weaving in and out of amblers who apparently had nowhere to be. A clump of chauffeurs huddling near the departures doors turned and straightened as the mass of deplaned passengers approached. Near the back stood a tall man in black trousers and a white starched shirt holding an iPad that read *Dunlap*. We made eye contact, and I gave him the obligatory chin raise, to which he nodded and stepped through the throng.

"I'll take your bag, Mr. Dunlap."

I grinned and patted the strap on my shoulder. "It would be more trouble to untangle it than to just keep carrying it."

He gave me a tight smile, then another nod, before turning and leading me out the door toward his waiting black sedan.

"Straight to the park?" he asked as he opened the back for me to toss in my bag.

For the briefest moment, my inner twelve-year-old wanted to make a crack about going "gaily to the park" rather than "straight" there, but some shred of adulthood—and likely a dose of dignity—responded, "Sure. I'm already late."

He grinned at the unintended challenge. "I'll see what I can do about that, sir."

The tires screeched as we rounded the last turn out of the airport, and I wondered why I'd thrown down the punctuality gauntlet and just which limb it might endanger. The driver never looked back. With two gloved hands on the wheel, he leaned forward, a grin parting his lips, as he wove in and out of highway traffic, barreling toward my destiny with a new team and his personal checkered flag.

We pulled into the stadium parking lot at four fifty-eight.

"No way," I muttered, glancing down at my phone.

My driver grinned and leaned back with one hand draped over the front seat. "Right on time, sir. Can't have the newest Clipper showing up late on my account. Give 'em hell, sir."

I shook my head and smiled. "I'm Nick, Nick Dunlap."

The gloved hand stretched back, so I shook it.

"I know. Center field, three-oh-one average last season, zero fielding errors. I could rattle off your minor stats, but those made the head-lines. We're lucky to have you, Mr. Dunlap. Team needs a strong bat and a golden glove."

An uncomfortable laugh escaped. "Not sure my glove is golden, but I appreciate the encouragement. I'll do my best. It's good to be a Clipper."

"Aye, aye," he said, saluting with two fingers to the short bill of his black cap.

The locker room was nearly empty as I strode toward a locker bearing a freshly painted label that screamed "Dunlap" in white on powder blue paint.

"Hey," the deep tones of a *surdo* rumbled from the corner, where I found a player leaning over the wooden bench, lacing up his cleats.

Brown eyes blinked up at me beneath two perfectly coiffed black brows. I tried to stare into them, to ignore his ridiculously perfect hair and chiseled jaw, and the five o-clock shadow that begged to be nuzzled and nibbled and licked. Believe me, I really tried to politely maintain eye contact, but perfectly bronzed arms bulged against the piping of his jersey in ways I'd never seen on a teammate. Our uniforms were meant to be worn loose, to allow freedom of movement, but his clung to him like that woman on her raft in Titanic. I could see the arteries or veins or whatever major roadways were flowing down his biceps into the curve of his elbow and down his forearm. Holy crap, I wanted to travel that road.

He cleared his throat, and my eyes snapped back to his.

"Oh, hey," I said artfully.

"You must be Nick. I am Marcus, Marcus Silva. We are the room-mates."

Even his accent was sex. Thick and Latin, and probably uncut … shit … his *voice* was thick and Latin. It most certainly wasn't cut. Voices didn't get cut.

Although, I wasn't sure what he meant by "the" roommates. My little head was certainly coming up with ideas.

Fuck me runnin'.

How was this supposed to work? This guy might've been the hottest man I'd ever seen in the flesh—well, I hadn't seen his flesh, only his arms and forearms. Shit, now I wanted to see his flesh. It was all I could think about.

He smiled, and perfect, pearly white teeth lined up for inspection.

And my eyes widened a bit.

"Oh, uh, hey. Yeah. That's the name they sent me. Marcus. I mean, that's you, and you're him. I mean, you're my roommate, and I'm yours … your roommate. I'm not yours. Not like … shit." I hadn't felt nervous walking in. It was just another team, another locker room, but for whatever reason, I suddenly had the urge to pee all over the pseudo-clean floor.

His grin widened, and the slightest lines formed around his eyes. Then he stood and I drank in what must've been a six-foot-five glass of sweet gay nectar. I'd seen hotness—hell, I was a pro athlete—but Marcus was on another level. Like model meets bodybuilder meets suntan-bed salesman hot.

"First-day jitters with the new team? I get it. Just breathe in deep and blow it out," he said.

"I wasn't ... I mean ... I'm not ..." The team had nothing to do with my jitters in that moment. And fuck, did he have to tell me to blow it out? Although, since he'd decided to remind me, my brain fled to that place every ten-year-old Little Leaguer goes right before stepping up to the plate, and I nearly peed my pants, which would've been bad because they're white and I was about to walk onto the field in front of thousands.

He chuckled. "It is all good. We are not Nashville. We've got behind your back."

My mouth opened, then closed, then opened again. I was pretty sure he meant something other than what I was picturing.

He stood, grabbed his glove, and trotted toward the door that led to the field. "Make sure you meet Kervin and Zack tonight."

He turned and opened the door. The familiar rush of the crowd's pre-game roar washed over me, like the steaming water of a much-needed shower after a long workout. There was something in that sound, that encouragement of the masses, that calmed my every nerve and shot adrenaline through my veins, all at once. It was awesome.

As I buttoned up my Clippers jersey for the first time, I glanced down and traced the letters and stitching with a fingertip. Everything was new, unblemished, waiting patiently for me to make my mark. I'll never understand why, but in that moment, everything settled into place, and I knew I was home.

Two

Nick

Two base hits, three RBIs, and a double play from center.

It was a good night. No, it was a great night, especially for a new guy.

"Dunlap, what the hell?" one of the guys yelled as we barged into the locker room following the game. I whipped around, baffled by what sounded like a player annoyed at my contribution to our evening's victory, only to duck a second too late as three wadded towels slammed into my head and chest. A chorus of lighthearted jeers followed.

"Dude, that was *awesome*. Way to show up on your first night and blow the curve!" another chimed in, slapping me on the shoulder.

The first guy, the accuser, squared up to me. At six foot three, I stood above most, but this dude glowered down at me. "Don't fuckin' keep that up or they'll call you into the majors before the season ends. We need your bat, man. Clippers need Nick like you don't know."

The knot in my chest released as an awkward laugh slipped out. "Thanks, I think."

Number sixteen stuck his head between us; he had hair so tall and frizzy I was sure it could never fit into a batting helmet. "Dude, Tex *never* says anything nice. Take it and run. Quick."

I wasn't sure if it was Frizz's easy smile or the dragon-grunt that belched out of the giant who'd congratulated me, but I struggled to wipe the goofy grin off my face.

Then Coach appeared in the doorway.

Pedro Garzon was a legend. He'd spent ten years as a batting coach for two different major league teams before landing the skipper position with his first MiBL squad, where he'd spent the rest of his career, despite multiple offers to return to the bigs. Players respected him, even when his team struggled. He was tough and direct and took no bullshit, but was also known to be fair. Some called him a "player's coach," but I wasn't sure what that meant. Coaches carried a pen that could strike a player's career from the books. How could they ever be a player's coach with that kind of power? I supposed, after Nashville, anyone who took our needs into consideration had to be better than the alternative. Maybe Coach Garzon would prove my fears wrong.

Like a pebble tossed into a pond, ripples of silence made their way throughout the locker room as Clippers glanced toward the doorway where Garzon stood.

"Men, great game. Really great game. Get some rest tonight and do it again tomorrow, alright? This town could use a streak to believe in."

"YES, SIR!" sang the chorus.

"Dunlap," he barked.

I stepped away from the frizz and the giant to face him.

"Yes, sir?"

He eyed me a moment, then nodded crisply. "Fine job tonight. Welcome aboard. Do that every night and you'll have a career, a damn good one. You're boarding with Silva. He'll show you the ropes. Evans is our captain. He can help too. The rest are a bunch of idiots." Easy laughs rippled through the room. "Don't listen to them—and please, for the love of all things holy, don't drink with Javier." The laughter grew louder, and taunts were hurled at a player behind me; Javier, I assumed.

Coach turned and vanished out the door toward his office, leaving me standing in the middle of a smelly, sweaty mass of hyper-pumped men.

A whispered cheer replaced the laughter: "Dun-lap ... Dun-lap ... Dun-lap ..."

Then grew louder. "DUN-LAP ... DUN-LAP ... DUN-LAP ..."

I could barely hear myself think by the time water bottles emptied all over me, from every direction, from every player and manager and whoever else might've been in the locker room. Everyone was smiling and laughing. Everyone was so ... happy.

As if someone had pressed the *Matrix* button, time slowed. The water squirting at me morphed into perfectly rounded droplets suspended midair. Players' mouths hung open at some yet-to-be heard jab. Stilled Clippers smiled and laughed, grinned and teased. Everywhere I looked, I saw brothers. There wasn't a single frown. No one glared or glowered. There wasn't one Santi among them; at least, none that I could see.

Part of me wanted to doubt, to question, to wonder if this would last, if this was how they welcomed every new teammate until they sucked or struggled or fell out of favor. Until they found out he was weird or different ... or gay.

Scanning the room through Gatorade-filtered eyes, there were no masks. The smiles were real and genuine and aimed at me.

At me.

God, it felt good.

Someone pressed play. "Hey, Nick, we're gonna grab dinner. Want to join us?"

I turned to find one of our pitchers, a painfully skinny guy with stringy blond hair that flopped to his shoulders, staring at me from two lockers down. I remembered the guys calling him Curve for all the obvious pitcher-reference reasons. The Clippers were welcoming. Original thinkers, they were not.

"Uh, sure. Sounds good."

"You don't have any weird eating rules, like no chicken or you only eat kale on Tuesdays?"

I chuckled. "I don't eat kale on *any* day, and that's a hard rule."

"You're in the club." Frizz appeared behind Curve, draping one hand over his bare shoulder. I hadn't thought my eyes could widen further, until he leaned down and kissed his temple, then returned to his locker to change.

"You, uh, might want to close your mouth. You look like a putt-putt clown with it open like that," Marcus chirped behind me.

My gaze shot from him and back to Curve, then back to him.

"They ... in the locker room ... those guys just ..."

He shook his head and grinned. "They're a couple, asshole. You better be okay with it too. We don't like dicks on this team."

My mouth snapped shut, but my mind continued spinning.

"Yeah, uh, I'm good with it. I mean, it's fine. It's good. Whatever works or makes them happy or whatever."

Marcus leaned in and motioned for me to do the same, then whispered, "I'm fucking with you, Nick. I know your story. I get it. Most of the team is straight, but we're cool. If you're one of us, you're one of us. Period. Relax."

I blew out a breath I hadn't realized I'd been holding, then nodded. "Thanks, Marcus."He slapped my shoulder. Shit, it was getting sore from all the team love.

"Come to dinner. It'll just be those two and us. Good chance to get to know each other."

I didn't mean to raise an eyebrow. It just shot up.

He raised both palms and chuckled. "I'm not on your team, but I'm a supporter, okay? Get changed. We'll grab food, then get you settled back at the apartment."

The quick ride across the river passed in silence. Marcus focused on the road, while I stared out the window, taking in the sights of my new city. It felt strange to be headed to dinner with some of the guys before even seeing the apartment I'd call home, but we were all tired and hungry and a bit hyped after a great game, like a kid who'd gotten high sucking down the pure sugary goodness of a Pixie Stick right before bedtime.

We followed as the guys turned into the parking garage of Gravity, a sprawling complex that made me think an office tower and shopping mall had a baby.

"Taft's is quick and easy. Good food. Great beer. You'll like it."

I grunted in the universal athlete language of assent. Marcus grunted back.

There was no wait. The brewhouse stood largely empty, but was filled with the scent of baked bread and fried food—with a hint of alcohol coating everything. It was the smell of perfection.

"Pitcher of your summer whatever. Don't let them order," the guy with the frizzy hair, who I came to learn was Zack, said to the server before I could even grip the menu.

Marcus leaned over and his cannonball shoulder pressed into me. "Just do whatever he says. He's good at this stuff, and it's not worth the argument—something he's bad at, by the way."

"I'm not bad at arguing!" Zack pouted more than replied.

Curve, who it turned out was so-named less because of his position and more because of his actual name, Kervin, flicked strings of hair from his eyes. "Babe, you're the worst arguer ever. Don't fight it. Just be zen."

"Zen? Seriously? That's your advice?" Zack scoffed.

"Everything's better when you're zen," Kervin said, as if it was a mantra written on marble tablets.

Marcus whispered, "Yes, they are always like this. You will get used to it. They are the best guys I know."

His breath was hot and smelled of bubblegum. I tried not to stare, but his lips were so close and perfect and red. Fuck.

"I am straight, by the way," Marcus said, and I tried not to let my entire body shrink, like some balloon being deflated.

Zack leaned over, his wild curls wiggling like a bad Jell-O dessert. "He says that because every man and woman alive wants to get in his pants."

My face must've turned three shades of red, because Kervin chimed in, "Hell, I'd do him, and I'm married to this fool. We call Marcus Apollo for two reasons. First, his throws from third to first are like an arrow shot. They're freakin' perfect."

"And second?" I asked.

"He's a Greek god," Zack answered without hesitation, and both the guys nodded and sighed. "It really isn't fair."

Marcus grumbled what I thought was a laugh. "Guys, I am right here. No need to talk about me ..."

"And then he has that stupid accent. You know, the one that makes you want to grab it out of the air, curl up with it, and make babies with it for the rest of your life?" Zack got a faraway look as he said the last bit.

Kervin blew out another sigh. "Yeah, all that. Apollo, can you just talk again? Say anything? Read the menu? Nothing sounds sexier than food in Spanish or Portuguese, whatever flavors your tongue. I haven't gotten off today, and I could use your help here."

"God, you two are terrible. What will Nick think of us?"

I chuckled, then handed him a menu. "Shut up and read. I'll get extra napkins for Kervin and me."

"Atta boy!" Kervin bellowed.

Marcus blushed as the guys and I lost it.

"Don't let him fool you, Nick." Kervin leaned over conspiratorially. "He might be our token straight, waving whatever boring flag they've stitched together without asking if the colors even matched, but he's *our* straight boy, and he loves the attention. Just when you think he's all offended and bothered, he'll crack a wiener joke that'll drop your jaw."

"If you had my wiener, your jaw might never shut again," Marcus snapped, right on cue.

My mouth flew open, Kervin hooted, and Zack just shook his head. The poor server chose that exact moment to arrive at our table.

"Did I hear someone wants sausage? We've got the biggest brats in town. We can barely keep 'em in back."

"So that is where you guys put those things," Marcus said in his most innocent voice.

And just like that, all three of us fell into a tear-filled fit, sending the server fleeing to the kitchen and my side aching long after he'd gone.

As we fought to catch our breath, I glanced between the guys. Kervin and Zack sat with shoulders touching, and, based on their proximity in the booth, I knew their legs had to be snuggled beneath the table too, likely with hands clasped. Every time their gazes met, time slowed. I could feel the energy between them, the obvious affection they shared with a catch of an eye. They were so light and free, as if the world existed around them, had been crafted about their union, and the two of them were all that truly mattered.

Pride, wrapped in envy, cloaked in regret ... yeah, that's what I felt warring inside me. Roiling and raging, straining at the seams of good conscience. I loved seeing a couple, especially two men, sharing special moments. There hadn't been many gay couples for me to look up to growing up. Hell, there hadn't been many successful couples at all, male or otherwise.

My own folks fought like ... like no kid should ever see.

I was eight the first time I watched my father dragged out of our home, dropped to the dirt, cuffed, and driven off in a cop car. It happened three more times before he vanished for good. I'd just turned fourteen. He'd missed my birthday, but he hadn't missed my mom's cheek. The only present he left for me came as stitches and a scar that would mar her perfect skin forever.

"Hey, you're up." Marcus's voice shook me free of my memories, and I looked up to find the server returned, pad in hand, tapping his pen impatiently as he awaited my order.

"Oh, sorry, black and blue burger with mushrooms, medium, fries."

"And to drink?" the server asked.

"Oh no. He's having what we're having. A pitcher of Under the Mango Tree and four mugs," Zack cut in.

"Mango beer?" I asked, trying to hide my disgust.

"Just trust me. It's ridiculous. And no, it's not nearly as fruity as I am, if that's what you're wondering."

Kervin giggled like some prepubescent girl, then leaned over and pecked him on the cheek. "My little mango." "*Dulce Jesús*," Marcus muttered beneath a smile that belied any possible annoyance. "They will give us all the diabetes before the season's over."

I was starting to get Marcus's speech pattern. There was something adorable about how the stunningly perfect man continually misused English phrases or inserted "the" where it didn't belong. I was no grammar hawk, but I found myself waiting for the next little gem every time his mouth opened.

"So," I decided to steer the conversation a bit. "How long have you two been together? Pretty unique, having a couple on a team."

Kervin shrugged. "Not as unique as you might think. It's the open, public nature of our relationship that makes us different."

"Oh, babe, we're different for a lot more reasons than that." Zack lowered his head and shoved his brown curls into Kervin's face.

"True. Very true," Kervin chuckled, and waved his hands like he was swatting flies. "We've been together three years, right before Zack graduated and got drafted."

"You met right before you got drafted?" Something in that astonished me.

Zack nodded. "Nah. We'd known each other for a year, played together, but we didn't hook up or anything until a few weeks before I graduated."

"I don't know what we were waiting for," Kervin said.

"Right. I mean, shit, we could've been screwing a whole year. It's not like I wanted anybody else."

Kervin rolled his eyes. "With me around? Of course you didn't. Admit it. You loved me before you loved me."

I swore I could see the smart-ass comment forming, then Zack leaned over and kissed Kervin tenderly. "I did, and I do. Forever, babe."

Zack's hand flew up to cup Kervin's cheek, then he said, "Me too, babe. Forever."

"Fuckin' diabetes. Shit," Marcus muttered, and the moment shattered.

Zack flicked Marcus a bird, then turned back toward me. "What about you? Bet you have a line of men crying their eyes out back in Nashville."

I blushed a little and shook my head. "Nope. Not a one."

Zack's brow furrowed, and he started to say something, then clamped his lips shut and nodded slowly.

"Two brats and a black and blue," the server singsonged as another uniformed staff member held our dinners on a large circular tray. The moment plates hit wood, we attacked. Either Marcus had understated how good the food was at this place, or I hadn't realized how hungry all-day travel followed by a baseball game had made me. My burger, slathered in blue cheese, crispy applewood bacon, caramelized onions, and sautéed mushrooms was almost enough to make me forget the slab of beef sitting beside me.

Almost.

Marcus let out the most sexual groan, and all three of the gay guys' heads snapped up.

"What the fuck, Marcus?" Zack asked. "Do that again and we're all gonna come in our jeans."

"Is alright. I already creamed mine. This brat is worth a lot of cream."

"I have ten different jokes on the tip of my tongue about you savoring a sausage, but I can't get the image of your creamy jeans out of my head long enough to tell them," Kervin said through a pantomimed pant.

Marcus shrugged. "Many people admire my cream."

I nearly spat a mushroom across the table.

"Maybe even a few at this table." The sly grin climbed to Marcus's eyes as Kervin began wagging a finger in the air.

"Don't you go planting dirty thoughts in my head. It took me a good year to accept your stupid straightness, and now all you do is tease us by flashing your tits or perfectly rounded ass. It's not right. There should be a law against—"

"Against what? Showing my straightness in public? Haven't your people fought for decades to enjoy the PDA? That's what you call it, isn't it?"

Zack snorted. "His people? Is Kervin Moses now? Did we lead a bunch of fags across the rainbow bridge or something?"

"Fags is such a nasty term. Can't you be nice to yourselves?" Marcus chided.

I'd kept my mouth safely hidden behind a mug of frothy goodness, but Zack decided to pierce my protective veil. "You. Stop hiding and come to our defense. Your brothers in arms ... with arms ... brothers who like arms ... whatever the fuck we are. We need you!"

I blew foam out of my mug and set it down. "You're so on your own, guys. I'm the rookie here, remember? I can't be seen to take sides in a family dispute."

"I am not disputing anything," Marcus said seriously. "These boys defame their rainbow heritage. I merely beg them to respect the path walked by those before ... in their open-toed sandals and chiffon."

The server, timing impeccable as ever, arrived and nearly spilled a newly filled pitcher all over the guys as he caught the last of our jabs.

"I either need to hide in the kitchen or pull up a stool, I'm not sure which," he said through gasps.

Kervin didn't miss a beat, shoving Zack over and patting the bench beside him. "Put that cute little tush down and join us."

The server's blush deepened. "I would ... really ... but my boss ... here." The pitcher thudded against the table. "Drink that, and I'll be back."

"I think you scared the little rabbit," I said to Zack.

Kervin snorted. "He acts so tough on the field ..."

"Hey! I am tough," Zack protested.

"JJ, with hair like that, tough isn't quite the word I'd use." Marcus grinned, then downed the last of his beer. I later learned the guys nicknamed Zack "JJ" after the character in the 1970s sitcom *Good Times*. I decided not to tell them that JJ didn't actually have a big afro since everyone, including Zack, seemed to enjoy the moniker.

Waves of chocolaty curls jiggled as Zack wiggled his perm. "My hair is my trademark. Don't be jelly."

I chewed my burger and tried not to make eye contact, sure it would paint me as a target of whatever silliness might come next. It turned out, my hiding was for naught—the target found me anyway.

"So," Kervin said through a mouthful of fries he stole off my plate. "What do you think so far?"

I quirked a brow.

"About Columbus and the Clippers?"

"Oh." I washed my bite down with some beer. It was surprisingly good for an ale with such a fruity name. "I've been here, what, five hours, maybe six? We played a game. That was great, then I ended up here with you guys."

"And we're awesome. Go ahead, you can say it. We can take a compliment." Zack wrapped an arm around Kervin and the pair batted their eyelashes like they were legs in a chorus line. I swear they must've practiced that maneuver.

I coughed a laugh. "Yeah, you guys are alright. Definitely a different vibe from Nashville."

Marcus lowered his voice. "We heard about some of what you dealt with. It's why we wanted you to come out with us tonight, to let you know you're part of a new family here."

I looked from Marcus to Kervin to Zack. The snarky humor had drained from each of their faces. All I saw then was sincerity and purpose. They really had planned all this to make me feel welcome. Something in that made me fight a lump from forming in my throat. I grabbed my beer and chugged.

"Easy there, tiger. That stuff'll kick ya if you drink it too fast. It's not like that watery piss you're used to." Zack raised his glass in salute, then took a ladylike sip and set it down, I guessed to show me how it's done.

I tipped my mug back and downed every last drop, then smacked my mug down on the table. "Another?"

The wind nearly escaped me as Marcus wrapped an arm around my shoulder and squeezed. It felt like some overly muscled anaconda had wrapped itself around my body and was determined to squish the life out of me.

"I like this one. He will be the good roommate, I think."

Kervin chuckled. Zack snorted. I tried to catch a breath while swooning at the musky scent of ridiculously hot Brazilian wafting from his armpit. Until that moment, I'd never been into pits. I made a mental note to revisit that later.

"The good roommate would like to breathe, please."

Marcus laughed, then squeezed tighter. My face had likely turned some variation of blue by the time he released me and slapped a meaty palm across my back, knocking the last of my air onto my nearly empty plate. I gasped.

"Looks like somebody's aiming for a toaster," Kervin whispered in a conspiratorial tone.

"Twenty bucks against," Zack shot back.

"Toaster? What is this? We just ate burgers." The confused look on Marcus's face only encouraged the cads.

"Twenty bucks, deal," Kervin said. "Toaster by spring training."

"Guys!" I said, surely blushing to the tips of my ears.

"I still do not get this toaster deal. And for twenty dollars? Is that expensive?"

"Marcus," I leaned into him and whispered loud enough for the boys to hear, "they're betting I can turn you gay by spring training. The toaster is an old joke from when you got a prize for opening a bank account."

"I am not gay, and I already have a bank account. I do not—"

Kervin and Zack burst out laughing.

I shook my head. "I know you're straight. It's just a joke. Don't worry about it."

He nodded, but I could tell by the way his brows still knitted he had no idea what we had just said. The server saved him from further torture, delivering the check, which Kervin promptly snatched while Zack wiggled a reproving index finger.

"We've got the new guy on his first night. He can buy the rest of the season," Kervin said as he dropped cash on the table.

"The rest of the—"

"Look how white he turned! Isn't that cute?" Kervin elbowed Zack, and they both chuckled.

Marcus rolled his eyes. "That was the joke."

I couldn't stifle a laugh, but turned and offered a respectful nod. "Thank you, Marcus. At least someone at this table has some class."

"You just don't know him yet. Rico Suave over there is as trashy as the rest of us, especially when he's drunk. If we didn't have that thing at the Ranch tomorrow, I'd get him trashed and show you what you've been missing. You might even make progress on your toaster project, too."

"I already have the toaster," Marcus said, still baffled.

Kervin slapped his forehead. Zack grunted, "The toaster's for rookie over there, not you. You're what gets cooked."

Marcus scrunched his brow further. "But, how would I fit—"

Kervin and Zack lost it again, so I stepped in to save my poor roomie. "What's the Ranch?"

"What?" Zack asked.

"You said you had a thing at a ranch or something. What's that?"

"Oh yeah. You should come. The Buckeye Ranch is a place—several places, actually—where they help kids with home life or addiction issues."

"Babe," Zack cut in. "They do a lot more than that." He turned back toward me. "These people are saints. They serve, like, two thousand kids—more, actually—with issues ranging from addiction and abuse to struggles with LGBT bullying and so much more. The team's been supporting them for years. It's my favorite community thing we do."

"Sounds pretty amazing," I said.

"It is, but it's not for the faint of heart. Some of the kids have really been through it," Kervin said.

"They're still going through it," Zack added. "That's the whole point of the place, to help them through whatever.""Here's your change. Have a great night," the server said, interrupting the conversation. Marcus stood, and the rest of us took the hint and scooched out of the booth.

Unsure how to say goodnight to my new teammates, especially in public, I reached out a hand to Zack. He and Kervin exchanged a glance, then both their mouths quirked up. Before I knew it, the two of them were wrapped around me in a three-way hug.

"Do not leave me out. I want the toaster too," Marcus said. His beefy arms enveloped us, and the guys began snorting loudly in my ears.

Three

Nick

"I don't have that much stuff, just some clothes, really," I said as I struggled to wedge my duffel through the doorway to Marcus's apartment—my new apartment.

"Really?" Marcus asked.

"Yeah. I never had much back in Nashville. You know how it is. The minors doesn't pay enough to go crazy, and you never know when you'll have to pack up and move—at least you hope you'll have to."

He shrugged and dropped onto the tattered couch that looked covered in burlap more than comfy fabric. "Guess so. I have been here my whole minor career, from Low A all the way to the Triple A."

I tossed my duffel onto the bed of the room he'd indicated, then flopped down beside him on the couch. "How long have you been on the Clippers?"

"I got moved up middle of last season, so a little over a year."

"You should get picked up soon."

He raised a brow, then dropped it. "I would hope. My arm is strong, and I am a solid fielder, but my batting average is ... how do you say ... holding me back."

I nodded. "I get it."

"You are not going to be here long. Your BA is solid, and you are even better in the field. We'll be lucky to keep you through the opener next year."

I blew out a breath with a laugh that sounded like a fart from my mouth. Marcus's head snapped toward me, then his lips curled.

"We'll see. I just moved. Literally just put my butt on this couch. The last thing I want to think about is moving again. Oof!" I grunted as Marcus slammed a cushion into my chest. "What was that for?"

"We would both move ten times in a week if it meant playing in the majors. Do not bullshit me. I am a bullshitting one."

I laughed and tossed the cushion back. "Yes, I believe you are."

"That wasn't right, was it?" His eyes dropped.

I suddenly felt really guilty for laughing. "Marcus, I'm—"

"Do not apologize. I will never learn the English if someone does not teach me when I drop the ball."

I suppressed another chuckle.

"Okay, well, I just want you to know I have your back. You're my roomie. It's you and me against the world, alright?"

He turned and squared his shoulders to me on the couch, raised a bushy brow, which I was coming to learn was an important gesture to him, and said, "Thank you, Nicholas. If this is not some attempt to win your bet with the boys, I appreciate it."

"Whoa, bet? What bet?" I raised both palms like a cop had me in his sights.

"To turn me. They are always talking about getting into my pants or pounding my man-pussy."

I spat-coughed-laughed. "I promise, I'm not chasing your man-pussy."

He wheeled around and stuck his ass in the air. "Is nice man-pussy, no? Why would you not want it?"

Dear god, save me.

"Marcus, put your ass back in its holster, please."

"But—"

"Yes, you have a nice butt. Hell, you have a nice everything, but you're straight, and I respect that. I want you to know I have your back ... as a roommate ... as a friend. Period."

"Period? This is a woman-pussy thing, is it not?"

"Marcus!"

He burst out laughing. "Just kidding. Sometimes I like to use what people think of me against them."

There was an evil, playful glimmer in his eye that made my heart thump in an entirely unwholesome way. I turned away and thought of root canal therapy. Please, horrifying dental work, please. Make it stop.

The warmth of his palm enveloped my shoulder. "You are a good roomie, Nicholas Dunlap. Welcome to Columbus."

Without another word, he rose and vanished down the short hallway into his bedroom and closed the door.

I took my semi-hard dick into my new room and did what frustrated players did when presented with a meal they weren't allowed to eat—and tried not to think about my hunky, bronzed, ridiculously sexy roommate as I did so.

Fuck my life.

I smelled bacon. My stomach growled. Then my bladder nudged my morning wood and my eyes fluttered open. One glance at my phone elicited a groan of "what the fuck," before I rolled off the mattress and staggered into the bathroom ... only, it was a closet.

Shit.

I was in a different apartment.

My new apartment.

Why was I smelling bacon?

My brain and stomach refused to coordinate their senses, so I opened the door and wobbled out. What had been a dull scraping appeared to now be a full-on whisking of eggs. Marcus, wearing an apron emblazoned with the words "Hot Crossed Buns" and no shirt—damn him—glanced up and waved his whisk toward my waist.

"Good morning, roomie. Did not know you wanted sausage with the eggs, but I can try to cook that if you really want."

I stopped cold, then glanced down.

Shit, I was naked. I'd walked out without shorts. Was I sleep-walking or just a moron? I was so not used to this roommate thing. Or was it mornings? I'd had a roommate before. And I swear I'd had mornings too, but they were a blur.

"Looks like is growing. Happy to see me? Aww, that is sweet," Marcus teased as he dipped his whisk again.

"Oh, god," was all I managed before turning and bolting back into my room, slamming the door behind me.

A rumble of Latin laughter seeped through the crack, and all I could think about was him dipping his whisk into a totally different crack.

"Sorry," I yelled through the door. "Just throwing on shorts."

A second later, I emerged in blue shorts that covered my skin but did little to hide just how happy I was to see Marcus.

He glanced down, smirked, then let his eyes roam up my body.

"Your chest is nicer than Kervin's, but I am still straight. Nice try."

Hell, I hadn't put on a shirt. This morning was not starting how I'd planned. What was I thinking? There was no plan. Clearly, I needed caffeine or something.

"Sorry, I just—"

"I am busting the balls, Nicholas. Relax. Come get coffee. Looks like you need it."

Not trusting my mouth to cooperate any more than the rest of me, I nodded and made my way around the counter to the coffee maker, where a full pot of blessedly strong java and an empty mug waited. He'd even set out sugar, Splenda, and two kinds of creamer.

"You're going to make someone a wonderful wife one day," I said as I poured.

He grunted and shook his head. "Always man-pussy with you boys."

I blanched. "No, Marcus. I didn't mean—"

He glanced over his shoulder, shit-eating grin firmly in place. "Got you again. You're easy, Nicholas, you know that?"

I sipped my coffee, savoring its richness and strength, trying not to think about how strong Marcus was, even though his rippling back was fully exposed to me.

"Yeah, sorry, not a morning person." I scanned the counter at the buffet he'd laid out. "Wow. Thanks for cooking breakfast. This looks amazing."

He dumped the last of the eggs into a bowl. "Cannot have my new roomie starving on his first day. Besides, I *am* the morning person, and

I like to cook. Plus, I have been to the Ranch several times, and they do not feed us much. We need the good breakfast."

"Thanks, mom," slipped out without thinking.

"You are welcome, son," he said, without hesitation, and I realized Marcus was far sharper than anyone gave him credit for—something he clearly used to his advantage.

"So, what's this place like? What do we do there? The Sounds were involved in the community, but more press conferences, fundraisers, and hospital visits. Easy stuff."

He spooned eggs onto his plate, then created a mountain of bacon. "There will probably be five or six of us. One will speak to whatever group is there. Then we will break up and just talk with the kids in a big common room with lab coats watching."

"Really? Like a supervised visit?"

He nodded. "Very supervised. They say it is not, but, you watch, it totally is. Some of these kids have been through terrible things. Some are angry. The staff watch for our safety as much as for the kids'."

A jolt of nervous energy shot through me at that.

"Really? You think we could get hurt?"

He shook his head. "Nah. Look at us. We are big. They are kids. I think the staff go overboard because we are like ... um ... celebrities."

I nodded and let that wash over me. Celebrities. Such a weird thing to say about yourself, but I guessed it fit. We might not have made it big, but we'd made it a lot further than most.

Marcus inhaled his massive plate of food, then glanced at my barely eaten eggs. "Down your hatch. We need to leave in thirty minutes."

"Oh, shit." I scooped eggs into my mouth as quickly as my fork would move. "I just need a shower."

"And pants. Do not forget pants. The kids will not appreciate your morning wood as I did." He laughed all the way into his room.

Just like that, my wood wiggled.

Marcus drove us south along I-71 just beyond the edge of town. We hadn't completely left civilization, but I could see farmland spreading golden in the distance, and only one side of the road still maintained the suburban sprawl of uniformed streets and houses. We exited the highway and traveled a short distance to stop before the gated entrance to a large, grassy tract of land. Thick trees lined the winding driveway, mostly obscuring my view of distant buildings, but I could still make out a perimeter fence that stood taller than our outfield wall. Its top was curved inward, clearly designed to keep guests in as much as to keep unwanted visitors out.

"Who do you think will be here?" I asked, unwelcome nerves beginning to bubble inside my chest.

Marcus shrugged. "The usuals. Kervin and Zack always come. Before the day is over, you will probably hear them talk about adoption."

"Shit. Really?"

He nodded. "They talk a lot. Just nod and tell them how nice it would be."

I chuckled at how he wrapped a matter-of-fact statement in thickly accented sarcasm.

"Tex and Cap will probably come too."

"Cap? Really?" Clark Evans, our team captain, seemed like a decent guy based on our brief interaction the night before, but he hadn't struck me as the kid-loving type.

His head didn't turn, but the corner of Marcus's mouth quirked upward. "The guys on this team will surprise you, usually in the best ways. Every one of us wants to make it into the majors, but I think part of us also hates the idea of losing any member of our family."

"Huh," was all the profundity I could muster.

We stopped before a second, stronger-looking gate and were challenged by a woman's voice crackling through a metal box.

"Welcome to Buckeye Ranch. Are you boys with the team?"

I craned my neck, searching for the camera that clearly had us in its sights. I found three in various positions above the gate—and another in the tree to our right, tucked high in the branches where it would be easy to miss. Oddly, it was pointed back toward the fence, not at our car.

"Yes, ma'am. This is Marcus, and I have a new player, Nicholas Dunlap."

"Alright. Come on back to the rec building. We'll get Nicholas papered."

Buzz.

The gate ground open on truck-tire-sized wheels, like some sliding patio door made of metal and gears rather than glass. Marcus drove through, then turned left into a small parking lot that sat opposite a one-story building that reminded me of a Florida ranch-style home.

It seemed silly that I felt nervous, but no matter how hard I tried, I couldn't stop fidgeting with my fingers. As he shut off the engine, Marcus glanced over and grinned again.

"Relax. Is a meet-and-greet with kids. Most of them worship players. The ones who do not will hide in the corner and glare."

That sounded more ominous than the ones fawning over us, but Marcus turned and crawled out of the car before I could ask anything.

As we strode across the lot toward the main door of the building, I drew in a deep breath. Fresh, almost sweet air filled my lungs. We weren't that far from the center of town, but something out here felt—and tasted—cleaner, more wholesome. Fall had arrived, and there was a crispness entering the wind. I could barely hear the cars on the interstate. Carpeted land stretched beyond the building, and I could hardly sense the ever-present cloak of a city's buildings and crowds. Then the scent of freshly cut grass drifted by and my mental respite began in earnest.

Until we walked through the door.

The sound of dozens of children of various ages assaulted us, only a second before a tow-headed boy who looked around five slammed into my leg and wrapped his spindly arms around me with the grip of an iron vice.

Marcus looked from my shocked face down to the elated boy and howled.

"Taylor!" the alarmed voice of a middle-aged woman called out, snapping the boy's head, but flipping whatever switch was required to release his clamps. "Let that man go. Don't make me come over there."

Taylor glared across the room at the exasperated woman, then massive pools of blue found their way up to me, and my heart lurched. Without thinking, I mussed his hair, and the brightest smile bloomed across his face. He gave my leg a last squeeze, then released me and ran back to his pack.

"I think you will do okay here," Marcus said, his eyes twinkling as he watched the interaction. "Only child? Really?"

I nodded, but kept my eyes on Taylor. He glanced back and waved from across the room. I found myself waving back—and grinning.

"Not anymore."

The woman who'd called for Taylor reached us before I could ask what he'd meant.

"Marcus, welcome back. Who's the new victim?" She smirked, and my roomie mirrored her mischievous grin.

"This poor soul is Nicholas. He was traded to our team yesterday, and is the new roommate."

Her smirk twitched, then her gaze snapped to me. "Welcome to Columbus, Nicholas."

"Nick," I said. "Please, call me Nick."

Marcus's meaty paw patted my shoulder, guiding me toward the side of the room to a small writing desk. The woman followed. We had to step over and around children playing with every sort of toy.

She nodded. "Alright, Nicholas. Let's get you papered. Let me apologize in advance. We ask for a lot of information of our guests: ten years of residency, employment information, references, several forms if ID, that sort of thing. This will take a minute."

"Oh, okay," I said, fumbling for my wallet. "All I have is my driver's license."

"And you're out of state," she said, snatching the plastic from my hand. "That adds a few forms. You'll be alright today, but make sure you bring one of these with you next time you visit. We also run background checks, so make sure to include any arrests, bankruptcies, things like that." She shuffled through a stack of papers on the desk and handed me a sheet with a list of acceptable forms of identification.

"Wow. Sure. I mean, I don't have anything to list . . ."

Something in the corner moved, and I peered around to find a few older kids watching us closely. Some of their glares weren't terribly warm.

The door chime sang, and we turned back to see Zack and Kervin enter. They'd made it a step or two inside before a whole team of kids bounded into them, tackling them both to the floor like a pair of quarterbacks getting sacked by the whole line ... and everyone on the sideline ... and in the stands. I could barely see our teammates under the mass of wriggling arms and legs, and the laughs and shrieks that flowed from the pile filled the hall.

"Yep. Zack is here," Marcus grunted.

"I'm not rescuing those two. They deserve whatever they get," the woman said with delight in her voice. She motioned toward two chairs. "Come, have a seat. Let's get you checked in. Marcus, you can go help untangle that mess if you like. I can take care of Nicholas."

"Just Nick is fine," I said.

Marcus shrugged and turned, then shot back over his shoulder, "Behave, Nicholas."

I shook my head. Clearly, there would be no easy victories.

"He's a big softie." The woman's sigh drifted, along with her eyes, to follow Marcus as he sauntered away. I had to admit, his ass in those jeans was a sight worth seeing.

"So, um"—she cleared her throat, clearly as flummoxed as I felt—"if you lend me your driver's license, I'll make a copy while you fill these out." She slid a clipboard with several forms and a Smurf-topped pen attached. I twirled the wild pink-haired character around before removing the cap and getting down to business.

By the time I set the pen down and retrieved my ID, several adults were wrangling the kids into a semblance of a semi-circle on the opposite end of the room. Kervin, Zack, Marcus, and Cap huddled against the wall, chatting quietly.

"We're all done here. You can go join the boys if you like," the woman said.

I smiled and handed her the clipboard. "Is it okay if I sit here and watch? I'm the new guy, and—"

Her hand found my arm. "Of course. Just relax."

Another middle-aged woman took the stage, tutted, and, in some feat of matronly magic, the room quieted. Introductions were made, though by the cat-calls of each player's nickname from the crowd, I doubted they were necessary.

The kids beamed as Cap stepped up and started speaking. He stood confidently before his awestruck audience, offering motivational words about doing one's best, staying in school, keeping away from drugs, all the usual things a public figure might tell kids in a talk. He was a natural leader, and the room belonged to him the moment his mouth opened.

Then Kervin and Zack stepped forward, as though one Muppet couldn't speak without the other, and the serious tones of Cap's invocation devolved into a comedic stand-up of third-grade bug-ger-joke-filled proportions. I knew those two were funny and unpre-dictable but had no idea they could hold court like that. Every time Zack wiggled his dandelion do, a group of the youngest young'uns seated in the front row would giggle and squeal with delight, as though he'd performed some mystical trick involving sugary treats and adorable puppies.

Marcus remained a statue beside Cap. I wanted to be frustrated by his lack of emotion or buy-in to the kid thing or whatever, but struggled to get past how much he looked like a Roman statue, effort-lessly chiseled, fashioned from nothing into sheer perfection. Then I remembered he was my roommate—my *straight* roommate—and forced my eyes to wander away from his nipples as they pitched two dreamlike tents across his chest.

I was so screwed.

I turned my attention to the kids. Adorable was an understatement for the munchkins in the front row. Their smiles broadened and their eyes twinkled every time Kervin or Zack said or did something silly. And their giggles ... sweet Jesus, who doesn't love the sound of a four-year-old's laughter? I thought my heart might burst right there.

As the rows flowed outward, so did the cuteness level. Children ranging in age from six to sixteen sat cross-legged, straight-legged, and downright sprawled, with seemingly no order or reason behind their posture. Most maintained reasonable attention, chuckling at their younger peers or something insane the guys did, but a few let their eyes drift to Marcus or a window or furtively toward a door I assumed led to an exit beyond the fence.

Despite the gravitational pull of the front of the room, I couldn't stop studying those in the middle and rear of the pack. What I saw was more than posture. It was more than *seeing* anything. The further back the rows went, the more the children felt distant and removed. Like a swelling tide, a wave of sadness flowed backward until it crashed at the feet of one lone boy. I'd seen him earlier, but hadn't really noticed him. He was slumped in a folding chair, head rested against the back wall, arms crossed tightly against his torso. His legs were spread carelessly before him, but even they held tension, a wary readiness, as if he knew a moment would come when he would need to flee. I watched him gaze out the window. There was defiant indifference in the set of his jaw, but something else I couldn't place.

I guessed the boy's age around sixteen or seventeen, though his eyes looked older, somehow colder. A hint of goth crept across his gaunt face, but without all the makeup and black clothing, and I wondered what stones blocked his path. From what Marcus had said, every child here struggled with something: the loss of one or both parents, some kind of addiction, depression, anxiety, perhaps a dash of each. Maybe one led to the other, then another? Who knew? None of it made sense to me—except for the sadness—the way so many of the kids' eyes turned down at the corners without the slightest effort or thought. It was just the way they'd been trained to curve at this point in their short lives.

My heart suddenly ached for them.

The baritone notes of Marcus's voice brought my attention back toward the far end of the room. He stood before an enraptured group: boys who clearly dreamed of growing up to be as manly, and girls who dreamed of his statue on their wedding cake—or whatever young girls dreamed about when presented with the most delicious dessert ever made by any chef, ever.

Fuck, I had to get a grip. I was daydreaming about smearing sugar all over my roommate. This was so bad.

"... and we were lucky enough to pick up a rising star yesterday." Shit. He was about to make me speak. "Everybody, welcome our newest slugger, all the way from Nashville—Nicholas Dunlap!"

The kids cheered and applauded on cue, and every head in the room snapped back toward me. I wanted to tuck my head down like a turtle wearing a baseball jersey, but I painted on my best celebrity smile and waved.

"Thanks, everybody. Glad to be here."

I was such an idiot, sounding like I stood before a room of boosters rather than kids.

Marcus smirked. Thankfully, everyone was staring at me, so I was the only one to catch his scorn.

I chanced a peek out the corner of my eye and noticed Mr. Sullen against the wall, trying not to get caught looking away from the window. For the briefest moment, he glanced toward me. Maybe he was curious about all the cheering. Or maybe, just maybe, there was a chink in his armor.

I wasn't trained in social work or psychology. The only thing I practiced was groundies and batting. Why was I suddenly keen on cracking what looked to be the hardest nut in the room? Why did I think I was qualified—or that he would give me any more attention than he had the other adults in the room that day?

It felt stupid when I thought about it, but something in my gut told me—

"What did you think?" Kervin and Zack bounded toward me, dodging tiny speed bumps as they wove through the dispersing crowd.

"You guys are a riot. They loved you."

Zack wiggled his hair. "The do is magic. Kills 'em every time."

Kervin elbowed him. "It was my jokes, idiot. Your hair does nothing but catch birds."

"You love my hair. Just last night you said—"

"Save me, Nick. Now. He's about to go where no child should ever go, if you know what I mean."

"So not those curly—"

"Oh god. You're on his side." Kervin threw up his hands and wheeled about, practically running back to the front where Marcus and Cap were entertaining youngsters.

Zack howled. "I'll pay for that later, but it was totally worth it."

"Glad I could be of assistance, m'lord." I offered a mocking bow.

"And he knows I'm a gentleman deserving respect. I think I'm gonna like this new teammate of ours." His smart-ass grin widened.

I choked out a laugh. "What do we do now?" He looked up as though I'd spoken in French.

I cocked a brow. "What?"

"What do you think? Talk with the kids. Hang out. Relax." He waved around the room. "We're here for them."

Two boys from the front row toddled up and grabbed him, one on each leg. Zack cried out like he'd been attacked, then did the monster march thing, forcing each kid to cling to him tighter or be thrown off as they moved awkwardly back toward the meeting area. The three of them laughed the whole way.

Unsure where to turn, I looked back to where the loner had been seated, expecting to find him staring out the window, but he wasn't there.

Four

Nick

I turned to scan the room for my missing mystery kid, but a reed-thin boy whose head reached my chest had crept up and now stood before me.

"Oh, hi there," I said, failing to mask how badly he'd startled me. The corners of his mouth edged slightly upward, but he didn't speak, just stared.

I waited.

He kept staring.

"I'm Nick."

His lip curled further upward, and one skinny palm raised in a wave. We stood no more than a stride apart, yet he waved silently.

I glanced up. The other kids were either huddled around other players or amusing themselves. The staff were busy supervising the mayhem. No one was watching us.

I kneeled so our eyes could meet as equals.

"What's your name?" I asked.

His mouth opened, then closed. His eyes fell to his feet, and his spindly arms clutched an even spindlier chest.

I waited.

"Okay, I'll guess."

His eyes shot up.

"Oscar?"

He squinted, assessing, then shook his head slightly.

"Adolphus?"

His mouth twitched, and something akin to life flickered in his eyes. Another head shake, this one a bit firmer.

"Let me think." I made a show of scratching my scruff. "How about ... Periwinkle?"

A giggle escaped his lips, followed by an emphatic head shake. His arms unfurled and hung limply by his sides.

"Those are all fun names, but I'm running out. Can you help me?"

He scrunched his brow, considering. Then his mouth pried open and one word croaked out: "Ethan."

I cupped my ear, as though listening down a well. "I'm sorry. It's loud in here with all the kids and goofy baseball players. Did you say Elmer?"

He giggled again, shook his head again, then gave me the universal *adults are so silly* expression.

"Ethan." This time more than a whisper.

"Oh, Evan. Got it."

"No, goofy, it's Ethan," he said, full voiced, then remembered himself, and his arms flew to grip his chest once more.

"Ethan! That's such an awesome name. I'm just Nick. Kind of boring, really."

He suppressed a third giggle, but I saw it in his eyes, in the way his clenched jaw released. He *wanted* to smile.

"Do you like it when we come to visit, Ethan?" I asked.

He nodded emphatically.

Kervin and Zack's voices were getting closer, so I glanced up. Several staff were dispersing the kids, sending them out into the sunshine of the playground just off the common room. Our visit was nearing its end.

When I looked down, Ethan had darted halfway across the room, where he slammed into a male staffer. The boy startled, looked up at the staffer, then turned back toward me and waved again. I watched him bolt out the door and into the brightness of the day.

The staffer, a man with flowing hair more gray than black, cocked his head. His eyes hid behind thick black glasses, but no amount of optical magic could've hidden the depth of his gaze. My heart lurched, and I found myself staring pointedly at my own shoes. When my spine returned and I looked up, he was gone.

"Ethan likes you."

I nearly jumped over the table.

"Holy sh—Oh, sorry, cr—Jesus, I shouldn't say that either."

I turned to find the silver staffer standing behind me. He smiled at my distress.

"I did not mean to startle. *Pardonnez-moi*." A thick French accent wrapped me in its warmth.

"Uh, sure, no worries."

"Did Ethan speak?"

Huh. That was a weird thing to ask.

I shrugged. "A little, yeah."

"What did he say?"

Now this felt creepy. The guy, handsome as he might've been with his lab coat and thick almost-beard, had yet to even introduce himself, yet here I was, getting the third degree on a monosyllabic conversation with a child.

"Well." I scratched my chin. "He called me 'goofy' when I guessed his name a few times, then told me his name was Ethan."

"That's all?" The man's unreadable expression hadn't changed since he'd snuck up on me.

"Yeah, that's it. Then he ran away, right into you."

Finally, he smiled.

Sweet Jesus, his smile ...

"I'm sorry for all the questions. That's the most he's said to anyone in months."

My jaw dropped, his smile forgotten—almost. His accent, though, was unforgettable. It was a warm croissant next to piping hot coffee and a cherry Danish, all on a winter's day looking out of a warm café at a snowy lane lined with ice-covered trees.

Wait, I'm a jock, not a poet. What the fuck?

He nodded. "Ethan suffers from a childhood form of PTSD. There is technical language for it, but that is the gist." When he said "the," it came out "*ze*." I had to stifle a chuckle.

He cocked his head again—ever the therapist, the assessor.

"Sorry, your accent—"

"I know." He lowered his head. "It is difficult for—"

"It's beautiful."

He blinked.

His hand raised to scratch his beard, then fell, as though he'd thought better of the gesture. "*Merci*."

A hint of a smile brightened his face. I had to flick a bead of sweat before it rolled down my neck.

"I'm Nick," I said, sticking my hand out to shake, unsure of the proper first meeting protocol between a child doctor or therapist or counselor—or whatever he was—and a non-patient-visiting baseball player.

It all sounded so odd when I thought it out loud … in my head.

"I am André Martin. It is a pleasure to meet you. Thank you for taking time to visit our children. Forgive me, I must get back to them."

I stared after him, open-mouthed, as he strode across the room to stand beside a thirtysomething woman in a matching lab coat.

"What did you think?"

I startled for the hundredth time that day.

"Shit, Kervin, can you give a guy a warning? Make a little noise or something?" I wiped my brow.

He and Zack laughed. "Why so jumpy? Got the hots for Dr. Mc-Dreamy?"

I rolled my eyes. "We were just talking—"

"Uh-huh. That's how it starts, you know. Next stop, babies," Zack declared.

My eyes nearly bugged out. "Babies? We barely shook hands."

"Ooh. You touched. It's fate. I can see it now. They'll have twins, and their kids will play with our kids. We'll grow old watching them play from the porch and—"

"You're impossible. I don't even have a porch. I live with Marcus."

Kervin sighed. "And then there's Marcus."

Zach echoed his sigh. "Yeah, there he is."

We all turned to watch the hottest player ever to don a baseball jersey saunter up to us.

"That was great. These kids are the bomb and shit."

Kervin slapped his forehead. "Wow. Just wow."

Zack and I snickered.

Marcus raised a bushy brow. "What?"

Five

ANDRÉ

"Out with it," Sara whispered urgently as my eyes roamed our charges.

"Out with what?" I asked absently.

She blew out a breath. "I saw you fawning over that new guy. He's cute. Like, really cute."

"Oh stop," I hissed, a touch too harshly. "Sorry, I saw him with Ethan and wanted to know if he spoke."

"The player?"

"No, Ethan."

"Oh. Did he?"

"Yes."

Her head snapped toward me. "Wait, Ethan spoke to a stranger? He won't even talk to us."

I nodded. "Yes, he spoke to the player. His name is Nick."

Her lip quirked up. "Nick is cute."

"He's a baseball player. It does not matter how cute he may be, he's stupid and self-absorbed. He probably would never visit here—or help anyone other than himself—if his team didn't demand a show of supporting the community."

"Ouch," she said, feigning a stab wound. "Frenchie has his foie gras in a bunch this morning."

"You know I hate it when you call me that ... and foie gras doesn't bunch. It is not small clothes. It is a delicacy."

She smirked and crossed her arms. "Forgive me, *Monsieur* Pépin."

"That's *Chef* Pépin, thank you very much." I wrinkled my nose at her in the most mature gesture I could think of in the moment. "Ethan speaking is ... I did not see that coming, especially not with a stranger."

"No, that's something. How should we follow it up?"

"Very casually. I will find an excuse to see him and ask what he thought of the visit. Perhaps this is a beginning, no?"

"We can hope."

Silence lingered as we watched the last of the kids filter out of the room.

"And how will you follow up with Nick, the self-absorbed cutie who was most definitely interested in ruffling your uptight, foie gras-stained beard?"

I scoffed. "My beard is not stained. Foie gras would not stain. And there is nothing to follow up with. We will likely never see the man again."

"Mm-hmm. Twenty bucks."

"*Quoi*?"

"Don't go all continental on me, Frenchie. Twenty bucks says you end up seeing him again, and soon."

"Fine. Twenty bucks, as you say. It will be your loss."

"And I want you to make me foie gras when I win."

I couldn't stop a grin. "I would make you a French meal anytime, with or without gambling on a hopeless cause. But be warned, your plain American fare will never taste the same once you've had the perfection that is the French cuisine."

She turned to leave, sneaking a snarky glance over her shoulder. "I know, but I want to taste my victory as you tongue yours."

"Sara!" I protested as she vanished down the hallway. The door slammed shut.

"*Merde*," I muttered under my breath.

Only a couple of the older children lingered, chatting away at a table on the far side of the room, so I dropped into a nearby chair. I didn't know how long I'd stood in that spot and watched Nick with Ethan. I'd been too far away, with too many kids in between, to hear or even see much, but it had felt like the longest one-word conversation I'd ever witnessed.

We'd still not identified a triggering event for Ethan's silence. Sometimes there wasn't one. Sometimes, a child simply reacted to a memory or thought. They shut down without warning, with no opportunity for us to intervene. That's what it looked like with Ethan. One day, he was a reasonably happy, if occasionally sullen, eight-year-old boy. The next, he was stubbornly silent, refusing to even speak with his peers. Before, he'd been drawn to adults, seeking us out in a room full of children, eager to chat or listen or simply be around us. For weeks, his silence had also cast a net about him, broadening his personal space from inches to miles. It was as if he wanted to run from any other human and hide, mentally, verbally, and physically, and I couldn't figure out how to reach him.

That left a nagging question.

Why Nick?

From what I'd observed, the player had been almost as reserved about the children as Ethan was with everyone. He'd smiled and waved on cue, but made no move to abandon the safety of the far side to interact.

That meant Ethan must've approached him.

"*Non*," I muttered, hardly believing it.

But that was the most likely explanation.

So, how had Nick, an untrained athlete, coaxed a verbal cue from my most stubborn patient? That was as much a mystery as the boy's silence itself.

My mind followed a familiar path, examining the evidence, analyzing the information available. Nick's face flashed to the fore, and the room became uncomfortably warm. I glanced around, half expecting to see it filled with children again, the heat of their overactive bodies a plausible explanation for my sudden flush. Alas, I was alone, the final two girls having abandoned their table.

I returned to the image, to Nick's thick brown hair and the curls that refused to stay neatly tucked, no matter how many times he pushed them back from his forehead. He seemed so irritated by them. I found myself smiling at that.

"*Arrête tes conneries!*" I chided myself.

Then my mind roamed down to where his broad shoulders and impressive chest pressed against the fabric of his jersey. I'd always been a sucker for a set of pecs, and he had a fine set, from what I could see. His biceps were a clue to that. They rounded nicely, popping out for a peek every time he reached across himself, or up... or down... not that I had been watching him or anything. I was a professional observing a stranger with a patient. That was all.

Though, it was a nice observation.

So, in my most professional inner-voice, I concluded Nick was hot.

That still did nothing to explain why Ethan had approached him.

Perhaps the boy loved baseball? Or dreamed of being an athlete?

Given his birth, that was unlikely. Oh, he might harbor those dreams, but his stunted growth would never catch up to dreams of athletic grandeur. Even he was mature enough to recognize that limitation. Other children born of an addict suffered far worse physical fates, but his limitations were sad enough.

Like the trigger for silence, sometimes there was no apparent explanation. Things simply happened. Without knowing Nick, or anything about their supposed conversation, there was no real way for me to diagnose what had happened with any accuracy.

That sounded clinical, even in my mind. Was I deflecting? Avoiding? Trying not to think of milky brown pools staring at me, or thick, corded arms wrapping around me?

I shook my head free. Nick was a professional athlete, lost to his own world, his own glory, his own desires. We'd seen the last of him when his teammates had hauled him away, and that was that.

I was sure of it.

Six

Nick

We caravanned back into town, three cars pulling into the lot of a Chipotle as the early afternoon sun tipped over its peak. My mind wouldn't stop spinning. First, the mysterious loner in the corner, then the young kid who gave me his name and ran. What was I supposed to make of those two?

"You've been quiet," Marcus said as we wheeled into the parking space beside Kervin and Zack's Toyota something-or-other.

I shrugged and stared out the window, watching the guys climb out. "Guess that place gave me a lot to think about."

When I turned, Marcus rested a hand on my shoulder. "It will do that. I am glad to see you taking those kids to heart. A lot of players show up and wave, then never think about them again."

I reached for the door handle. "Thanks. I don't know how anyone could look at those faces and not ... I don't know ... be moved or something."

"That is profound ... or something," he smirked, then shoved me out the door.

I held the restaurant door and shifted my attention from the children of the Ranch to those standing in line for pseudo-Mexican goodness. On a minor leaguer's salary, fine dining involved any restaurant with cutlery, plastic or otherwise, served rolled in a linen napkin or in a plastic bag you had to rip open. The latter was what we were more used to. Shrimp forks were overrated.

"Nick! What did you think of the Ranch?" Cap stuck out his fist for a bump, then dove into some elaborate team captain handshake ritual that lost me halfway through. He ended up slapping my fist with his open palm twice and calling it a shake.

"Uh, good, I guess. Kervin and Zack were a hit."

"Of course we were," Zack said, threading pride with defiance.

"Duh. We're awesome. Every kid knows it," Kervin added.

"I think I liked you two better when you couldn't stand each other," Cap said.

My brows must've hit the ceiling because Kervin busted out laughing and pointed to my face.

Zack grinned. "Yes, we hated each other at first. When I got called up—"

"Guys, she asked you, chicken or steak," Cap interrupted.

"Oh, sorry. Steak for me."

Kervin added, "Chicken. Love me some chicken," then pinched Zack's butt and made him jump.

"Hey!"

"My little chicken," Kervin quipped.

"Is going to peck you right here if you do that again."

"Promises, promises."

I turned toward Marcus, who'd snuck into the back of the pack. "Are they always like this?"

He shook his head. "Usually worse, especially when the whole team is around and doing the egging."

I cocked my head. "Egging?"

"The egging of them."

I stared, then it struck. "Egging them on?"

He nodded as I lost the battle with a muffled laugh. Cap leaned in and whispered into my ear, "He's the best guy on the team, but his English will keep you in stitches. I'm jealous you got to be his roommate."

"So's every gay man in town," I mumbled.

Cap stepped back. "What?"

"Nothing. Uh, I think it's your turn to order."

We finally made our way to the register, paid, then found a table. Pro athletes eat like a pack of wild animals, and our table was filled with so many wraps, bowls, and tacos of every variety, there was barely room for our drinks. In a blink, we went from a boisterous, jovial bunch to the quietest table in the place, Marcus's open-mouthed chewing excluded. His chomps could be heard in the parking lot.

"So, rookie, what do you think of the team so far?" I looked up from my chicken and bean bowl to find Cap staring at me. Humor had been replaced by thoughtful curiosity.

I swallowed my bite and washed it down with some tea. "Well, I've played one game with you guys, but we've barely spent any real time together. We seemed to click on the field. Guess you should ask me that after a few days of practices or, better yet, after a week-long roadie."

"Fair." He nodded, his brow still creased. "You stood in back the whole time today."

It was a statement made with the weight of a dozen questions.

I took another sip, an odd tingle creeping up my arm as I did.

"Yeah, guess I wanted to get a feel for how you guys do those things. Nashville was pretty ... I don't know. I wasn't really put on stage much." I hadn't meant to lower my head or stare into the salsa Marcus had spilled across the table, but I couldn't look up, couldn't let him see ... whatever.

"You're not in Nashville, Nick. We won't hold you back from the spotlight. In fact, you deserve the stage here."

I waited for him to go on, but he didn't say anything else. When I finally looked up, the others were staring but trying to look casual, while totally failing to not focus on my every movement. Hell, I thought Marcus might've counted my breaths.

"Okay, good to know. Thanks," I muttered in a small voice that reminded me of a certain boy who'd given me his name an hour earlier.

We ate in silence, something I was coming to learn was rare for these men, especially the couple sitting across from me. I couldn't take it.

"So, um, Zack. You said you two hated each other?"

His grin returned as he nodded.

"Kervin was such a pretty-boy shit. I couldn't stand the fucker."

"I can't help it if I'm beautiful," Kervin singsonged.

Marcus tossed a wadded napkin into his chest.

"He was pretty hot. I mean, he still is, but shit, when he first joined the team, I could barely focus." Zack peeked sideways at Kervin through his curls, like a kid peering through a thicket, and his smile brightened until it reached his eyes. "I didn't hate him, really. It was more like, well, I fell in love with him the first time he shook my hand, and I didn't know how to tell him. He was funny and sexy and everybody worshipped him. I was just this puffy-haired weirdo half the team didn't know was gay."

Kervin set his fork down and turned toward Zack. "Babe, come on. You're freakin' amazing."

Zack shook his head. "But you were the sun filling the locker room with brilliance and warmth."

Marcus pushed back from the table, muttered something in Spanish, then Portuguese, then barked in English, "God, I am going to hurl, right here, chunks of the salsa and the steak all over you two. Please, for the love of the baseball, the apple pie, and every fucking aunt who ever baked one, shut the hell up. We get it. You are in love. Gah!"

He snatched his empty wrappers and tray off the table and stormed off toward the trash can.

Cap doubled over, and I swear I saw a tear dribble down one cheek.

Kervin and Zack never broke eye contact, like they were in some kind of love time-warp and couldn't hear any of the hyperventilation taking place around them. It was sweet, in a diabetic, gorging-on-a-bar-of-pure-sugar-cane sort of way.

Cap finally sucked in a breath and wiped his face. "You okay with all this, rookie? There's no escaping these two."

I snorted. "I'm very okay with it. After Nashville, I guess I forgot what it was like being around guys who are just ... just who they are. I spent so much time worrying who might be offended by my presence that I forgot to live."

Cap leaned back. "Wow. That sucks." He eyed me a second, then glanced at Zack, who was *still* entranced. "You won't have that problem here. This team will make you be yourself, whether you like it or not."

I finished the last of my bowl. "That might take a minute to get used to, but I appreciate it. Thanks, Cap."

He saluted with his last bite of burrito.

"So," he said through a mouthful, "what's the story with you and Doc?"

My brows scrunched. "Doc?"

He gave me that *don't bullshit a bullshitter* gaze out the top of his eyes. "Dr. Martin from the Ranch. I saw you two talking after the thing. Looked like he was into you."

I snorted again. "More like into shooing me as far from his kids as possible. I'm not sure he likes baseball players."

"He likes us just fine." Kervin finally emerged long enough to throw shit across the table.

"Yeah," Zack added. "He's gay, single, handsome as hell, and crazy-smart. You should definitely tap that."

"And did you see his ass in those tight dress slacks? Every time his lab coat rode up, I felt a little flushed. Tap ... tap ... tap," Kervin said, wrapping a knuckle on the table with each of the last three words.

"Guys!"

"For once, the wonder twins may have a point. Tappy tap, rookie," Cap said.

"Cap! There will be no tapping, tappy or otherwise. Hell, I doubt there will be any talking. He *really* didn't like me, and I'm an expert in knowing when I'm not liked."

Cap crossed his arms again.

Kervin started to say something, but Zack's hand found his forearm, and they exchanged a silent glance that likely contained more words than a Dickens sentence.

Six eyes glared, then Marcus appeared.

"What did I miss? Did the roomie say something offensive or stupid? My money is on stupid. He's not the offending type, but stupid—"

"Um, thanks, I think. You managed to defend my honor while kicking me in the balls. Impressive," I said.

He shrugged. "Did not know your honor was on the table. Here, I will get the knife so I can stab it."

My eyes popped wide.

Zack lost it.

Kervin had to leave the table and laughed all the way to the restroom.

Cap stared, stone-faced.

"What?" I asked him.

He shook his head. "You might not be as good at reading people as you think, especially yourself, but that's something you'll have to figure out on your own. I've got shit to do."

He rose, gathered his things, and headed to the trash bin.

It was late in the afternoon when Marcus and I finally stepped into our apartment. There had been no practice or game. We hadn't even worked out, but I felt drained. Something about the trip to the Ranch left me weary, yet wanting to return. I had so many unanswered questions.

"You need anything?" Marcus asked as I reached for the doorknob to my room.

"What? Oh, no. I'm good. How are we stocked in the kitchen? I can make a run."

"I knew you were coming, so I went to the store yesterday. Take a look. If there's anything else you want, we can go together later. We're close enough to walk to almost everything."

That was good to know. My Nashville apartment was okay, but I had to drive twenty minutes to get to the grocery store.

"Sweet. I might actually take a nap first. Today really wore me out."

He chuckled. "The kids will do that. It was nice seeing you talk with Ethan. He has had the rough time."

My head snapped up. "You *know* Ethan?"

He shrugged. "Not really. I have tried talking to him, getting him to toss a ball or whatever. Doc asked me to last month when we were there. The boy would not even make eye contact."

"Huh."

"Anyway, you should go back to the Ranch if you have time this week. I know the staff have been worried about him, and you got his first word in weeks, maybe longer."

I nodded slowly, thinking. "Yeah, I'll try. What's a game day like here?" "You will see tomorrow, won't you?" He grinned. "We are pretty laid-back. Coach almost never practices on a game day, even when he is really pissed at us."

"Coach Garzon gets pissed?"

He snorted. "He is Spanish. Of course he gets pissed. He just hides it better than most."

"Great. I have a Brazilian roomie and a Spanish coach. I'm so screwed."

"You wish I would screw you."

My jaw nearly slammed into the floor.

Marcus burst out laughing, his deep rumble filling the room like a tuba struggling to anchor a discordant high school marching band.

"Sorry, it is rude to tease. I know I am ... how do you say ... the tasty treat."

And for what felt like the hundredth time in twenty-four hours, he spun and vanished down the hall, his hoots following close behind his perfect ass.

"I hate straight men," I muttered, trying to keep the smile off my face. I would not be amused by him and his abs and perfect smile and amazing chest and ridiculous sense of humor and insanely sexy accent. He would not win. I would not like him. I would not be attracted to my very straight, very welcoming roommate.

I wanted him so fucking badly.

I didn't nap. My hand took care of my Marcus problem, christening my room on my second official day of occupancy. Every time Marcus's face flashed before me, I'd swipe it away. Then his chest appeared, then his legs. God, he had tree trunks for quads. Then trees made me think of another trunk, an uncut one, full and plump and ripe for the picking ... or licking.

FUCK!

As I lay in the fruits of my own labor, something strange happened. Marcus vanished, finally.

And André's face appeared.

Seven

Nick

"Who names their team after a bat?" one of the guys asked loud enough for everyone in the locker room to hear. Half-naked men, and a few blessedly naked ones, sat on benches, strolled between the showers and toilets, and simply stood in all their professional athlete glory. Baseball was my passion, but there was nothing like a pro locker room to get one's eye candy juices flowing. I had to cover mine with a towel just to avoid a scene.

"They're the farm team for the Cardinals," another player answered.

The first one refused to let go. "So? A cardinal is pretty and red and ... nice. A bat is gross and scary. Shit, they're vampires."

"Hey!" another shouted from the opening to the toilets. "Vampires are cool."

"Really? Blood suckers?" the first one asked in disgust.

"Who doesn't love a good sucking?" the guy quipped before disappearing into the toilet area. The locker room erupted at that. Good-natured sucking jokes flew faster than baseballs on a diamond. The naysayer surrendered to the wisdom of the crowd and laughed along with us.

At no point in our getting-ready-before-the-game did anyone talk baseball or strategy or mention anything about our opponent du jour.

In my former locker room, it would've been the only topic of discussion. Coach insisted on "absolute focus," which meant there were no shenanigans until after each game, and only then if we won and played well, two things that could be mutually exclusive. Victories gained because an opponent fell on a sword of errors were not rewarded with joviality. They were examined, dissected, corrected.

This relaxed, almost celebratory pre-game ritual felt like walking through the streets of Paris for the first time. The buildings were all perfectly in line, beautifully symmetrical, colors complimentary. The language flowed and tickled the ear. The skies were clear and blue, the breeze sweet with the scent of baking and confectioner's sugar. With every step, every stride, the city welcomed and embraced. It was impossible not to fall in love.

Yet none of it made sense or felt real.

But what did I know? I'd never been to Paris, and locker rooms did not smell of sugar, confectioner's or otherwise.

Then I realized something patently obvious: this was the final week of the regular season. The Clippers were a decent team, but weren't close to making the top four spots, which meant there would be no playoffs. I wasn't sensing any pressure in the locker room because there *was* no pressure. These games were for pride, the fans, and building up individual stats hoping to catch a major league team's eye.

Nashville had been in the playoff hunt in each of the seasons I'd played for them. We were never allowed to relax our focus, much less our physical readiness. Every game represented a step toward or away from a trophy, bonuses for players and coaches, and the pride of the franchise. Every game carried weight.

For Columbus, the weightiest decisions, at least until next spring when the new season began, involved which restaurant would enjoy our company after the final out was called—and that was an entirely different pressure from the one I'd felt in Music City.

"You get your cherry popped or something?"

I snapped out of my daze to find Marcus looming, all of Brazil represented in his bulge that was eye level, just within reach ... of my mouth.

"Uh, hey, um, no. No cherries. No popping, I mean. Nope."

He grunted a laugh. "You are sure turning red enough. You sure someone did not sneak in the pop?"

By then, I'd gathered myself. "No, nothing that good. You'd be the first to know."

"Second. I am straight, remember?"

"A boy can dream, can't he?"

He crossed his arms. "You saying I am in your dreams?"

Shit, he was, but I couldn't admit it, definitely not here in the locker room.

"No, of course not, gross. I mean, you're my teammate."

"Hey!" Kervin, who I hadn't seen standing behind the Hulk, chimed in. "I fantasize about a teammate all the time. In fact, he pops my—"

"Guys! Shit, really?" I finished lacing my cleats and stood. "There was no fawning, dreaming, or popping with anyone, teammate or otherwise."

"Maybe there needs to be," Marcus mumbled to Kervin. The asshole snickered and nodded.

Ignoring them, I said, "I was just realizing this season is almost over. I just got here, and we're about to be done."

"Yeah," Cap said, joining the circle. "Way to slam the door on your way *into* the clubhouse. So much for helping us win a championship."

"I'm an outfielder, not a miracle worker. Babe Ruth couldn't have saved your season."

Towels, socks, and one smelly shoe slammed into me from every direction as the team unanimously expressed their displeasure with the new guy pooping on their season's accomplishments, few though they were. For the briefest moment, I thought I might've overstepped, but good-natured laughter, teasing, and backslapping erupted as the guys shoved each other toward the door that led onto the field.

I watched them for a second, then joined the flow as Marcus's meaty paw pressed into my back. "Go on, little one. Get in the pen. Time for play."

The heat of his hand sent my mind to a completely different kind of pen—and play.

Dammit.

As little as these last few games mattered in the record books, I knew, as the new guy, they would leave a lasting impression on the coaches as they evaluated each player's performance in the off-season. I needed to make my mark so there would be no question who belonged in their outfield come spring.

I batted fifth in the lineup, a strong position earned by my rock-steady batting average. In the first inning, I stepped up to the plate with two men on base and one out on the board.

The first pitch curved into the dirt, forcing the ump to replace the ball.

The second pitch nearly hit my shoulder.

The third sailed over the catcher's head, nearly decapitating the ump, before smacking into the stone wall and rebounding back toward the plate.

I was up three–oh.

The Nashville coaches would've waved me off, demanding I take the pitch in hopes of an easy walk. I glanced over toward third for a sign. My new base skipper pressed his thumb to his chin, then made a handful of senseless signs designed to obscure his real intent.

A green light? He was letting me swing?

I stepped a second foot out of the box and cocked my head, the universal *give me that sign again* signal.

Thumb to the chin.

Well, hot effin' dog. It *was* a green light.

I stepped into the box, tapped the plate, then turned toward the pitcher and wiggled my ass. The ass wiggle was my thing, like a goldendoodle hearing the word *walkies*; I'd done it since Little League whenever things got tense or exciting.

The pitch came in hot. A fastball.

SMACK!

The fat of the bat could not have been better.

The ball screamed over the pitcher's head, soaring higher and farther, sailing over the center fielder to slam into the wall just below the yellow line and bounce back into the field with verve. The center fielder misjudged the carom, giving the men on base time to trot home and me time to round for third.

My second game, my first triple, and two RBIs.

Fuckin' ay!

In the fourth inning, we were up 7–0, crushing the Bats. I knocked the ball into the left outfield corner and made it safely to second, driving home another RBI.

Three. Three ribbies.

In the seventh inning, when normal people stretched and sang, I stepped back into the batter's box. After six foul balls, my seventh contact landed me on first. Cap had been on third and tapped a toe on the plate for my fourth RBI.

By the time I stepped up in the ninth inning, we were leading 16–0. In most games, when the score is out of reach and the game is late, fans flee for the exits to beat the traffic. But it felt like more had arrived. The place was alive and rockin'.

I took a ball, then a strike, then dug in and wiggled my butt.

Someone near the front row yelled out, "Here it comes. He wiggled!"

I tried not to laugh.

In came the pitch. Another fastball.

And the fat of the bat ...

The ball sailed over everyone, over the fans in the left-field stands, over the restaurant and the massive monitor, and vanished into the parking lot, where a car alarm bleated.

There was a split-second of silence, then the stands went wild.

Shouts of "Dun-lap, Dun-lap" swelled as my toe struck second, and I thought my heart might leap out of my chest.

The third-base coach smacked my ass as I rounded toward home, and the entire dugout emptied to greet me. Marcus squatted, wrapped his arms around my legs, and hurled me into the air like some gymnast sending his partner flying to the roof. Other players joined in, hefting me over their heads and marching back toward the dugout with my arms and legs flailing, and me giggling like a ten-year-old who'd just gotten his first kiss.

I'd played in the Little League World Series, for a high school state championship team, and on one of college baseball's dynasties, but in all my time on the diamond, I'd never felt anything like that night.

We were a middle-of-the-pack team, already eliminated from playoff contention, but none of that mattered.

Anyone watching would've thought we'd just won the World Series.

Hello, Columbus.

Eight

ANDRÉ

E than stared into his clasped hands tucked between his legs. His feet were tucked beneath his folding chair, interlocked and clutched tightly. He didn't have to speak. His body was screaming at anyone who would listen.

"How was breakfast, Ethan? I saw the compote on your plate. Was it good?"

Yes, I was resorting to asking about food. Sara and I had tried everything we knew, every trick of the psych trade, and now we were tossing Hail Mary passes at the poor kid, desperate to find something—anything—that might spark life into his eyes. Outside of a one-word introduction to that baseball player last week, the boy hadn't spoken in nearly two months.

His eyes shifted from his hands to the window, then his entire body leaned and he rested his head against the glass.

"Do you want to go outside? I think a few of the others are out there playing basketball."

Nothing. Not even a twitch.

Sara thought he must've had a nightmare, some subconscious resurfacing of a horror from his past. If there had been a trauma within the facility, we would've heard about it. Even the best-kept secrets among our children reached our ears eventually. Everyone talked, especially to us. We specialized in getting people to talk.

I hadn't ventured a guess as to Ethan's "triggering event." I wasn't sure there had been one. Sometimes, the brain just takes a break, or, more appropriately, tells its human to take a break. At least, that's what I was telling myself. I wasn't sure if I believed that explanation either.

"Ethan, if you could have anything in the world, or do anything, what would it be?"

I'd almost given up when his head moved. Like a weightlifter struggling with an overloaded bar, he forced his eyes up toward mine. I gripped the pen in my hand, as a trickle of hope traveled up my spine.

But he just stared blankly, as if I was simply a different window.

My chest fell.

I was trained to not show what I was thinking or feeling, especially with a patient, but I couldn't hide my disappointment. We'd been so close. I could sense it. He *wanted* to answer.

What was holding him back?

Why couldn't he just open his mouth and respond?

I clicked my pen a few times in distracted irritation, then slid it into the spiral of my notepad.

"Okay, I think that's enough for now. Why don't you go outside and get some fresh air? It's nice today."

His only acknowledgment that I'd spoken was to rise and exit the door to the courtyard, leaving me to stare at the empty chair before me.

I rose and walked around my desk, tossing my pad aimlessly down before staring out the window. Ethan sat alone on the edge of the pavement, glaring away from the kids playing ball, at some indistinct spot beyond the perimeter fence.

"No progress?"

Sara's voice startled me. I hadn't even heard her open the door.

"I thought we were close, but maybe not. No, no progress."

I turned toward her as she blew out a sigh and dropped into the chair opposite my desk. She started to say something, but a *ping* followed by the crackling of the PA system stilled her voice. PA announcements were common, but the urgent voice of director Katherine Marber making them was not.

"Doctors Martin and Adams, come to the main office, stat. Code four. Repeating, Doctors Martin and Adams, come to the main office, stat. Code four."

Our gazes widened, then we raced out the door.

Nine

ANDRÉ

"Noah Riley is missing," Dr. Marber said to the half-dozen staff gathered in her office. "We've already alerted the local authorities, and our grounds team is canvasing the area."

Dr. Marber stood behind a massive wooden desk that looked like a lengthier version of the ornately carved Resolute Desk in the Oval Office. Her floor-to-ceiling drapes shimmered before sun-kissed windows that offered a view of the rolling, grassy landscape beyond. The walls were lined with old leather tomes tucked into rich wooden shelves, and her chairs and couch were covered in worn leather that gave the room both the feeling and scent of merry old England.

She probably wouldn't have enjoyed my psychoanalysis of her decorating choices, but I had to admit, it was grand.

She turned toward me. "Dr. Martin, you are Noah's primary. Thoughts?"

"We all know how troubled Noah is. When I heard the code, I feared he might've tried something worse than running." I ran a hand absently through my hair. "My guess is that he'll stay close to the Ranch. He would never admit it, but this is his home. He feels safe here, even if he resents all of us for locking him away, as he'd put it. I believe he is expressing his desire for more freedom, not actually running away."

Dr. Marber nodded thoughtfully, then turned to Sara.

"Dr. Adams?"

"I agree with André; he'll stay close. If he were an adult, I would suggest not searching for him, to let him come back on his own. Therapeutically, that would take him a few steps down the path toward ownership. As a minor, I understand that's not possible." Sara thought a moment, then added, "When we find him, it will be important he's met with someone he trusts, either André or me. If someone else on staff hauls him back, he'll view his return as an involuntary capture—and that will multiply in his mind if a policeman makes first contact."

"Agreed. I'll make sure the locals know to find him, but not speak to him, only observe." Dr. Marber uncrossed her arms. "Any thoughts on where he might go?"

I nodded slowly. "I have an idea. Sara, why don't you take your car and drive around? I want to change and take my bike out."

"Your bike?" Dr. Marber's arms recrossed.

I nodded again. "I think I know where he'll go. If he sees me on my bike, he'll just think I'm out riding. It'll be a less threatening approach."

The silent pause that followed was painful. Finally, Dr. Marber sat behind her desk and looked up.

"Okay, but if your way doesn't work, the police will have to take over. We can't have a ward roaming around out there. Keep me updated through text."

"Yes, ma'am," I said.

Sara and I exchanged a quick glance, then everyone scrambled to their assignments.

I lived across Hoover Road in a residential community called Meadow Grove. It was a typical suburban neighborhood with neat streets and fenced yards. The best part about living there was that I could walk to work on a pretty day. Driving home took less time than it usually took to get through all the gates of the Ranch in the morning.

A quick change and an apple for lunch later, my helmet was strapped on tight, and I was pedaling my way back toward the complex; but, rather than turn into one of the gated entrances, I turned south on Hoover Road and headed to the small shopping plaza that sat just outside the southern perimeter fence. Noah might've been a rebellious teen, occasionally volatile, but he was supremely predictable. If our theory about him sticking close to home held, there was only one place he would've gone.

The afternoon air was crisp, but the sun hadn't received the "it's fall" memo yet, and I was sweating by the time I rolled into the parking lot, cruised past Kroger, then Dollar Tree, then the local McDonald's. I broke all manner of pedestrian laws, taking the sidewalk west to parallel London Graveport Road. My stomach churned as I passed Flyer's Pizza. They served great pizza, but their subs were the best in town. Atop their building was one of those exhaust ports that blew the scent of freshly baked bread and Italian goodness into the neighborhood. It took all my willpower to ignore my nose and continue to the next building whose parking lot adjoined the pizzeria.

I heard Petland before I saw their doors. Several long folding tables had been set up on the sidewalk near the shop's glass entrance. Crates and cages filled with kitties, puppies, and a few rabbits lured shoppers into conversations around enlarging their families with furry friends. Petland hosted the local shelter two days each week, and this was Noah's favorite "off-campus" activity.

As I drew closer, the back of his head became clear, his messy, unmistakable black hair blowing in the breeze. Something furry and golden poked its head over his shoulder, and I watched as the angry boy gently cooed in its ear, lulling it back down into the warmth of his arms. He bent his head and nuzzled the pup with his nose. I hated to disturb the scene.

"Do animals always like you?" I asked quietly.

Noah didn't turn, just kept nuzzling. "Animals are easy. They want attention and love—and food. People are the fucked-up ones."

I grunted before I realized it had slipped out. "You're not wrong. People are more complex." I leaned my bike against a railing and snapped its lock into place, then stood and watched, giving him a few more peaceful moments.

"What's his name?" I asked.

"Callie. He's a she."

"Ah. Callie. Cute name."

"Card says her parents live on a farm in California. Guess they ran out of names like Ghost."

I grinned. "That one might have a trademark."

He glared over the knotty, fur-covered head, his eyes squinting. I couldn't tell if it was annoyance or amusement.

"What kind is she? I can't tell from her fur."

He rubbed her head, earning a few licks on his chin. "Card says she's a golden mix. Guess they couldn't sort her out without some kind of test."

I pulled up a chair, careful to keep us several paces apart.

"Are you here to drag me back?" His voice was anger wrapped in wry resignation.

"No."

That brought his head up, and our eyes met.

"I was out for a ride, saw you over here. At least, I thought it was you."

His eyes squinted again.

"Okay." I held up both palms. "The cavalry has been called, and I have orders to take you down, dead or alive. So, which will it be?"

He rolled his eyes. "Your sense of humor is overwhelming. They teach you that in head-shrinker school?"

I grinned. "We don't shrink heads. We crack them open. There's a clear difference."

He tried to hide it, but I saw his lips twitch upward.

"Noah, are you okay?"

It wasn't the way I would normally address a patient, but we weren't in my office or any other controlled environment. We sat in public, him holding a puppy he didn't own, on a sidewalk where anyone could hear our conversation. On top of all that, he was not a typical sixteen-year-old boy. He was highly intelligent, yet emotionally and socially stunted, a very complex, dangerous mix if handled poorly. Remove the sense of empathy on display in his arms, and he might make serial-killer-in-the-making profile.

Thankfully, he had empathy in abundance. He was a beautiful soul and a wonderful boy. He just needed to believe it—and address the issues from which many of his emotional struggles emanated.

I watched him wrestle with how to answer my simple question. Everything in me wanted to place a hand on his shoulder, to wrap him in a hug and tell him it would all be okay, but I knew better. He had to seek help, or at least accept it, on his own.

"I guess," he whispered.

"You guess what?"

"Guess I'm okay. Callie likes me. That's something, right?"

"That's something," I agreed.

A few moments passed in silence, save occasional barks and meows from neighbors still in cages hoping for a little of Noah's affection.

"Are you okay, Doc?"

After twenty years in the field, I wasn't often surprised, but Noah managed it almost every time we spoke.

"I'm better now. I was worried about you."

"Why?"

"I'm sorry, why what?"

"Why were you worried about me?" he asked. "There's a ton of other kids, probably easier kids to help—or whatever you do. Why worry about me?"

I started to answer, then froze. This was it. This was a pivotal point. He would either accept my hand or reject it—in this moment. I could feel the weight of his question on my chest. It was suffocating. I couldn't imagine how it must've felt for him.

"Noah, will you look at me, please? Don't put Callie down. Keep holding her. Just look at me."

Slowly, reluctantly, he turned. Callie, my beautiful accomplice, nuzzled his neck with her tiny wet nose, and I watched the tension in his shoulders release, just a bit.

"How long have we known each other, Noah?"

He scrunched his brows. "Eight—no, nine—years. That's how long I've been a prisoner."

I let the jibe go. "Nine years. That sounds right. In that time, we've spent hundreds, probably thousands, of hours together. What have you come to think of me?"

"What do I think about *you*?" Now it was Noah caught off balance. "I don't know. You're my doctor."

I nodded. "True. I am your doctor, and you are my patient. Is that all?"

Callie decided she wanted to squirm, and Noah had to fidget to get her to calm. Interestingly, he calmed more quickly than she did.

"I don't know what you want me to say. You're Doc Martin."

"I want you to say what you really think. What you feel. Who am I to you?"

He thought a moment. "I guess you're a friend too."

"What does that mean? What does being a friend mean to you?"

He went silent, focusing on Callie.

I waited.

Still, he didn't speak.

"What it means to me," I said, moving the conversation forward, "is that I care about you. Not your file, or your chart, or anything to do with the Ranch. About you, about Noah. You were just another patient when we met, a seven-year-old pain in my ass, truth be told."

His eyes flickered up, amusement dancing at their edges.

"Then I came to know you. Not the act you put on around other people, the real Noah. I'm not sure how many people you let see you, but I appreciate, more than you know, how you've let me in. It means a lot to me. You've become more than a friend, Noah, you're family, and I truly care about your wellbeing and happiness."

His eyes hardened, then drifted to the dog, then began to water; yet he remained silent.

I waited.

The sun was beginning to set, and the woman working the animal rescue tables started hauling equipment and fur balls to her van. Noah's time with Callie was ending.

He finally looked toward me again. "It's chicken fried steak night. I really hate chicken fried steak."

I chuckled, both at the change of subject and how right he was about the abhorrent concoction. French chefs died to give us cordon bleu and other masterpieces, yet Americans drowned their hunger in deep-fried beef and gravy. It was vile.

"Would you like me to cook you something else?"

He handed Callie to the worker. "They'd let you do that at the Ranch?"

I shook my head. "No, but you could come to my house for dinner. I would need to let Dr. Marber know where we were, and promise you'd come back on your own after we ate. Are you okay with that? With going back?"

Callie whined as her crate was carried past him toward the van, her eyes never leaving the boy.

"Yeah, I was going back when this closed anyway. Dinner sounds good. You doing some of that fancy French shit?"

I barked a laugh. "Only if you like fancy French shit. I could grill hamburgers if your neandertal American stomach demanded it."

"Whoa, Doc, big words. Easy."

His smile put me at ease.

"Let's head back and see what's in the pantry. You can choose what I make. Deal?"

"Deal."

We stood and I unlocked my bike.

"Hang on. Let me let Dr. Marber breathe again. She was pretty worried about you too."

He snorted. "She was worried one of her canaries escaped its cage. She doesn't even know me."

I wanted to argue, but he was right, and the last thing I needed at that point was to damage the trust we'd built with a lie he'd see coming from miles away. So, I turned and sent a text.

> **Me:** Noah is with me. We are getting dinner then will return. You can call off the search.

Noah chose not to choose, so the dinner choice was left up to me. When I whipped out ground beef and taco seasoning, he glared.

"Tacos? From a Frenchman?"

"I've been in the States for two decades. I think I'm allowed to cook beyond my borders."

He leaned against the pantry cabinet door and scrutinized my every move as I diced tomatoes, onions, and jalapeños and tossed them into the strained beef, then covered everything in beef stock and stirred in the seasoning.

As the meat mixture simmered, I shredded lettuce and grated cheese. When I pulled out a bag of Scoops, my guest stirred.

"What are you doing with those?"

I grinned. "Call this my twist on a classic. Each Scoop is a mini taco." He crossed his arms again. "You'll see. No messy taco shell to fall apart and scatter."

I spread Scoops out on a plate, then layered grated cheese, the meat mixture, fresh tomato, then lettuce. "The cheese on the bottom keeps the chip from getting soggy. Here, try one."

He reached out for the proffered sample like it had fangs and was about to strike; but the moment he started chewing, his eyes widened and a smile formed.

"Tastes like a taco."

I laughed. "It *is* a taco, Noah, just in a Scoop instead of a big shell."

"It's really good," he said through a mouthful of tasty non-French shit.

As we ate, we chatted about Noah's favorite television shows. He was a keen observer of *Survivor*, insisting my psychological training would serve me well if I ever "had the balls" to try out for the show. He hated *American Idol*, but knew every contestant, their style, and every song they'd performed throughout the season. The finale would air next week, and he was still upset that his favorite was cut in the last round. He argued there was a dark conspiracy behind the show and its votes, and that producers really decided who advanced, not voters. I shuddered at the parallels with the country's political reality, but kept the cork in that bottle. We'd made too much progress to spoil it on something as petty as American politics.

It was nearly eight o'clock when we strolled into the main building of the Ranch. Dr. Marber had left for the day, but was keeping tabs on us via text. The common area was mostly empty, except for Sara, who was working a late shift, and a few other kids milling about. Noah gave me a fist-bump, a *sup* head bob to Sara, then vanished out the door that led to the residential wing.

I finally breathed a sigh of relief.

"Rough day?" Sara asked rhetorically. I gave her a wan smile and nodded.

Visiting hours ended at eight, so I was surprised to see an adult sitting at a table in the far corner with one of our kids. The man's back was to us, so I couldn't make out who he was, but the kid was obvious. I nearly stumbled.

"Is that—?"

"Ethan, yes," she said. "He's been *talking* all night."

"*Merde!*"

"Exactly. You're never going to guess who got him talking."

"*La vache,*" I muttered.

My mouth was suddenly a desert filled with cotton balls made of barbed wire.

She snorted. "If he's a cow, he's the hottest damn cow I've ever seen. His shoulders fill out that shirt like you're not going to believe. And don't get me started on his chest. I hadn't realized how cold it was in here until his nipples—"

"Sara!"

"What?"

"Who *is* that?"

"That's Nick Dunlap—*your* baseball player."

Ten

Nick

Our season ended with a whimper, losing to the Norfolk Tides, the team with the worst winning percentage out of all the teams in both leagues. If it hadn't been for one struggling Single A franchise, they would've been the worst in all the minors.

And we lost to them; 7–0.

I committed my first fielding error with the Clippers and didn't step foot on base—unless you counted tripping over first as I ran toward the dugout after the fifth-inning side was retired.

That was almost as embarrassing as the scoreline.

In the end, I think we were all just glad it was over: the game and the season. It had only taken a week of playing with these guys for me to feel at home, to realize Columbus was a great place with even better people, but every player longs for the rest and recovery of the off-season. Our bodies take a beating over one hundred fifty games, many of which occur in cities other than our own, requiring endless travel and nights in uncomfortable hotels. The idea of sleeping in our own beds, making food in our own kitchens, and working out on our schedules—if only for a few months—was a blessed relief.

Marcus hadn't wasted any time, flying back to Brazil to spend his holiday off-time with family. I hadn't realized his flight was the day after the season ender, and was disappointed we wouldn't get to spend more time together. Set aside his annoying hotness, he was a great guy and was quickly becoming a brother. It felt odd to say after such a short time knowing each other, but I'd miss the big guy.

So, on the first day following the end of my week-long season with the Clippers, I sat alone in our apartment, drinking lukewarm coffee, staring at reruns of *Bewitched* in black and white. I checked the clock on the wall, suddenly worried I might be late for a morning practice, before realizing there were no morning practices until March—five months away.

I'd experienced two off-seasons in my career, but I'd been surrounded by teams I'd played with all year. There was always someone gathering a group for pickleball or cornhole or some other silliness, guys being guys and all. I didn't really know the Clippers well enough to make the short list for spontaneous activities.

I thought about calling Zack and Kervin. They'd hang out. Then I realized this was their first morning of the off-season, and I decided to let the happy couple have their first post-season morning together without my interruption. Cap would probably be out trying to save the world or something. The guy really did need to wear a cape.

That made me think of doing something good, rather than sitting there wallowing about doing something fun.

Ethan.

It had been a little over a week since the Ranch visit. I wondered how the boy was doing, if he'd spoken any more since we'd been there. He was a cute little guy, and I could tell there was a happy boy buried beneath whatever muck life had layered all over him. He just needed someone to help clean him off.

Dr. Swoopy Gray Hair decided to show himself in that moment, all swarthy and sexy in a tightly fitted lab coat that looked remarkably made of rubber. Wait, that wasn't my memory, that was the other part of my brain that created spicy dreams.

Gah!

I was trying to do good, not do *myself*.

Although a good doing might do *me* some good, then I would be in a good mood when I left my apartment to be a do-gooder.

And that was a lot of good going on.

Twenty minutes later, I shut off the porn on my iPad and padded into the bathroom, careful not to dribble any of the fruit of my labor onto our linoleum. A quick shower and change later, I was ready to tackle the day, then realized I didn't have a car in which to tackle anything. I hopped back onto my iPad and looked up bus routes in the city. There was one that went right to the Ranch. How convenient.

Nearly two hours and eight thousand stops later, the bus whooshed to a halt at the corner of Hoover and Pineville, the southeastern corner of the Ranch. I thanked the driver on the way out the door and trekked back up the street to the security gate.

It took another ten minutes to get through all the gates, convincing different members of the staff who I was and why I was visiting. They directed me to the community center, the building the guys and I had visited before, so I cut across the open, grassy expanse rather than taking the road on its L-shaped journey. It was a nice day for a stroll through a park, especially after being cramped on a bus for hours.

Dr. Sara, as she insisted I call her, greeted me at the door.

"Nick, what a nice surprise." She glanced over my shoulder. "Just you? No other players?"

I nodded. "Yeah, just me. Thought I might see Ethan again. How's he been?"

Her mask slipped a bit, then snapped back into place. "He's been fine. Hasn't spoken since you left, but he's been okay."

"Huh. Alright. Would it be okay if I saw him?"

She thought a moment, then nodded. "We don't usually let non-family members visit with the kids, but I think this would be alright. I'm covering the common room today, so it'll be a supervised visit."

I grinned. "Have you seen us in practice? My whole life is supervised."

She smiled. "Good. I'll let Ethan know you're here. Have a seat wherever you like."

As I scanned the room, my gaze landed on one lone chair in the corner where the older, sullen boy had sat. I made a mental note to ask about him, then made my way to a table set with two chairs against the opposite wall by a window overlooking two tennis courts with nets that looked like they'd seen better days.

Ten minutes passed, then twenty. I was beginning to wonder if Dr. Sara had forgotten me. Then the doors opened and Ethan followed her into the room. His eyes widened and face brightened, and a flutter filled my chest.

How could a child's smile bring me such joy?

He bolted from behind Sara and raced across the room to skid to a stop before the table.

"Hey, buddy. It's good to see you again," I said, grinning from ear to ear.

Ethan grinned back, but didn't speak.

Why had I thought the boy would be so happy to see me that he would simply start babbling? What was I thinking? Professional therapists and psychiatrists were practically begging the kid to talk, and here I was, a baseball jock, thinking my jersey and a toothy grin would win him over.

I was such an idiot. What was I even doing here?

"I ... um ... I'm ..." Ethan stuttered out, nearly knocking me over with a few simple words. "I'm glad to see you too."

Sara and I exchanged wide eyes. When I didn't move or speak, she made a shooing motion, encouraging me to keep casting whatever spell I'd used to get the little guy speaking. She quickly retreated, but not to her seat across the room. She landed a few tables over where she could eavesdrop.

Unsure how to proceed, I did what I'd seen Kervin and Zack do with boys his age: I reached down and mussed his hair. Brown strands flew in every direction then remained in place, like he'd stuck a finger in a light socket. The smile he gave me crawled into his eyes and creased his forehead. I thought my heart might burst.

"Why don't we sit down? I brought you a present."

I hadn't thought his eyes could get any wider, but he proved me wrong as he scooched his chair from the six o'clock position to nine o'clock. He sat with his legs tucked under, on his feet, leaned forward on the table as though he might leap across at any moment.

I dug into the small pack I'd had strapped to my back when I arrived and retrieved a game-worn ball and rolled it across the table toward him. He snatched it up in both hands, then tossed it into the air and caught it.

"That's the ball from last week—my first homer with the Clippers. I traded a fan a jersey for it because I thought ... well, I thought you might like it."

Ethan gaped up at me, his mouth forming the widest O any alphabet ever imagined.

Then he hopped out of his chair and threw himself into me, scrawny arms wrapping around my neck, squeezing with all the strength they possessed. His little face buried itself into my neck, and I felt, more than heard, him say, "Thank you, Mr. Nick."

I finally gathered myself enough to wrap my arms about his shoulders and whisper, "Just Nick, okay? My team's pretty worried about me getting a big head already. If they hear you call me mister, I'll never hear the end of it."

His giggle sent a shiver across my skin, and I swear someone was cutting onions nearby, because my eyes watered. I glanced over the boy's shoulder, hoping to find support in Sara's eyes, but one hand was covering her mouth and tears were rolling down her cheeks too.

I was an only child. There were no uncles or aunts to give me cousins, no brothers or sisters to give me nephews or nieces. I'd always been alone, without other children, until school and baseball, but those couldn't compare to the closeness of a familial bond—a bond I'd never experienced.

In that moment, as insane as it sounded to say in my head, I knew what that sense of family felt like for the first time. Ethan had given me that gift. My meager offering paled in comparison, though the boy seemed to think better of the ball than I did.

It felt as if something in my heart was cracking open, and I didn't even know what it was. I hadn't known there was anything *to* crack open.

Ethan finally pulled back.

He didn't return to his chair, just sat in my lap staring down at the ball. He spun it in his tiny hands, felt the laces, traced fingers over the pro baseball logo as if some god had emblazoned it from Mount Olympus. On that point, he might've been right. As a kid who'd always dreamed of playing pro ball, that indicium was as close to godhood as I could imagine.

"Nick."

He spoke with such reverence; awe I didn't deserve.

"Yeah?"

"Is this really your home-run ball?"

I nodded. "I wouldn't lie to you, buddy, not about baseball, for sure."

"So cool," he whispered, as if speaking aloud might end his dream.

"Are you ready for the other part?" I asked.

His head snapped up, as he gripped the ball against his chest and muttered, "There's more?"

I think every tooth I possessed was on display in that smile. Ethan's innocent enthusiasm made me giddy.

"One more thing, but I'll need your help to use it. Okay?"

His face sobered, as if I'd just asked him to take a hill from an enemy.

I reached down and pulled out a kid-sized glove. The leather was worn because I'd had our guys run it through some of the conditioning machines back at the park. The signatures covering the outside of the glove were new.

"That's every player on the team. I even got Coach Garzon to sign it, and he can be kinda grumpy."

Ethan tried to say "Whoa," but a giggle mingled with his wonder and he sounded more like a frog farting than an excited kid.

We both laughed at that.

I chanced another look at Sara to find our intrepid doctor, both elbows planted on the table, her chin resting atop them, gazing, bleary-eyed, in our direction. For a pro, she sure was emotional about this one. She gave me a thumbs-up then returned her chin to its resting place.

"I thought you might help me work on my groundies," I said, smoothing my face to look as serious as possible. "I had an error last night, and that can't happen again if I want to make it into the majors. Will you help me?"

Ethan thought a moment, his eyes darting from the ball to the glove, then his head rose and nodded. "You bet, Mr. ... I mean, Nick."

He threw his arms around my neck again, and I could feel the ball and glove pressing into my back. I pulled his head further into me with one palm, and savored the feeling of the boy's affection.

How could anyone not love this little man? I wondered.

When he finally pulled back and took his seat, any hint of the silent boy had vanished, replaced by a typical eight-year-old and his torrent of questions that threatened to sweep me into the parking lot.

"What's it like playing pro ball?"

"How far did your homer go? Was it a rocket?"

"Is a fastball really fast? Is that your favorite pitch? What's your least favorite? I bet it's a curveball, maybe a slider. Curveball, right?"

"Is Coach really mean? He looks mean. He's always frowning in the dugout."

"Are all the guys on the team as silly as Zack?"

"Why is Zack always with Kervin when they visit?"

An hour passed, then another. Sara had migrated back to her spot near the door, but was ever watchful as we chatted. Her delighted expression had yet to falter.

Every so often, Ethan would run out of questions, or would need to breathe, and I had a chance to ask him a few things.

"What's it like living here? Do you like the other kids?"

He shrugged and looked like a balloon slowly losing air as he thought. "It's okay. The food is good most of the time. I guess the kids are nice enough."

He paused, but I thought he had more to say, so I waited.

"They never stay here long."

"Who?" I asked.

"The other kids. Especially the younger ones. They get adopted or moved into a foster home. It's hard to make friends when they always leave."

I sat back and resisted the urge to cross my arms. I hadn't thought about the turnstile effect of a facility such as this. It seemed so residential and settled. Those were terrible words, but it's how I'd seen it. I'd been wrong.

"How long have you lived here, Ethan?"

His eyes dropped to the glove still glued to his hand. "Since I was four."

He was eight.

Half his short life had been lived in an institution.

Most of the younger kids got adopted or moved. Why hadn't he? He was a sweet kid, still young and impressionable, teachable. Most eight-year-olds might have a fairly settled personality and compass, but he'd been stunted, physically and emotionally. Did that mean he was more apt to take guidance, to evolve and change, or less? Were the worst of his ordeals behind him? Or would he struggle with a lifetime of hangover effects? Was an entire youth behind a fence more damaging to his long-term mental health than his birth? Or was that simply what a child in his situation needed?

I had so many questions but knew better than to ask the child. I'd have to talk with Sara before I left.

He'd turned serious, so I decided to steer our conversation back to baseball.

"How do you know what Coach looks like in the dugout?"

He gave me a blank stare.

"Have you been to a game? We're not on TV, unless you catch a super-rare news report."

He stuck out a proud chin. "I've been to a few games. They let us do field trips sometimes, with permission and all that. The team does a Buckeye Day every year too, and most of us get to go and sit together in the stands. It's my favorite day of the year."

In that moment, I was reminded of the weight of responsibility that rests on the shoulders of every pro athlete, whether or not *we* realize—or accept—it. Boys like Ethan looked up to us. They idolized us. We didn't deserve it, but it was reality. More than simple fandom, they watch and learn from everything we do. They are tiny mirrors of our actions. The example we set is reflected on Little League fields and in gymnasiums across the country and throughout all sports.

All we wanted to do was play a game and get paid, but our very existence helped influence how younger players acted and who they would become as athletes—and, in many cases, as adults. We weren't in their lives like parents or teachers or family—I knew it was silly to overstate our role—but we were a presence with power. These kids deserved idols who made them proud.

I thought back to how some of my former teammates acted on the field, the mini tantrums they threw when things hadn't gone their way, and I realized something: that was an example too. It wasn't one I was proud of, but it was what we taught our followers and fans that day.

Ethan deserved better. All Ethans did.

"I'm going to do better."

I hadn't realized I'd said that aloud until Ethan asked, "At what?"

"Oh, uh, sorry, was just thinking about the game, things to work on, you know?"

He scrunched his nose like he didn't believe me. It was cute.

We sat in silence for a long moment, him staring at the ball and glove, me lost in thought about everything I'd seen and heard that day.

"Why'd you come back?" His tentative voice startled me out of my daydream.

"Here?"

"Yeah."

"I wanted to see you," I said.

"But why?"

His eyes were lasered onto mine.

This moment mattered. It really mattered.

I sucked in a breath, desperate for a moment to think. "Well, because—"

"Please don't give me some dumb adult answer. I really want to know why."

My throat caught.

"Because I was lonely and wanted a friend."

His eyes widened as his chin rose. It was as if the boy was staring into my soul, weighing my words and deciding whether he believed them. It felt like the longest moment of my life.

"You? You were lonely? Really?"

I nodded, unable to speak.

"And ... you wanted me ... to be your friend?"

I nodded and gave him a tight smile. Any more would've threatened a brief moment of emotional stability. He didn't know it, but I was putty in that boy's hands.

He stared forever.

I didn't look away.

Then his hand left the safety of his new glove and rested on mine atop the table.

"You're my best friend, Nick."

Eleven

Nick

I had to turn away before the tears fell. One hand was held fast by Ethan's fingers, but the other flew to my face. My heart felt like it was full and swollen—and about to seize up at any moment. I desperately need a staffer to interrupt, or an alarm to sound, or cars to start honking outside so I had an excuse to stand up and free myself from whatever vice this boy held me in.

"Having a nice chat?" a heavily accented voice answered my silent prayer.

Ethan's head snapped around so fast I worried he'd hurt himself. I glanced up to find Dr. Martin—André—standing a few paces from our table. I'd been so lost in our conversation that I hadn't noticed him enter and had no idea how long he'd been standing there.

"Yeah, it's been great," I said, struggling to keep my voice level.

André quirked a brow.

"Ethan, it's time to get ready for dinner. The cafeteria only has thirty minutes before they shut down."

The boy nodded, rose, and took a few steps toward the exit. Then he froze. His back was to us both, but I could feel him thinking, deciding ... something. He wheeled about and darted into my chest, wrapping his arms around me once more.

As quickly as the hug began, he flew across the floor and vanished out the door, leaving a stunned André staring down at his even more stunned guest.

"That was ... unexpected," he said.

My wry smile put us on the same footing. "Have all French mastered the art of understatement?"

He chuckled. "You have us confused with the British. They are all clouds and curtsies. We are quite expressive."

André flipped Ethan's chair around and sat with his arms draped over the back, then motioned for me to join him.

"Dr. Adams tells me you have been here for hours."

I nodded.

"And Ethan spoke with you the entire time?"

I snorted. "He's a chatty little guy once he gets going."

André's smile wasn't convincing.

"What did you say when you first arrived?" he asked.

I cocked my head. "What do you mean? When Ethan first came out?"

He nodded. "Yes. This is important for his progress. I need to understand."

I shrugged. "I told him I was glad to see him—oh, and that I'd brought him a present."

André's other brow cocked. Was that a French thing? I wasn't even sure I could control both brows, at least not separately.

"I brought him a baseball and a glove, told him I needed help on my fielding work because I had an error the other night. I asked if he'd help me."

André leaned back, a thoughtful smile spreading across his face. Then he started chuckling.

"Something funny?"

His chuckle grew. "A baseball and a glove, from a baseball player, no less. That's brilliant." He clapped his hands together and began to laugh.

I still didn't get the joke.

He finally settled and asked, "I heard him ask why you'd come today, but couldn't make out your answer. What did you tell him?"

Now it felt like the therapy was aiming uncomfortably in my direction.

"Isn't that kid–player confidentiality or something?"

André laughed. "There is no such thing, but I applaud your creativity."

"Well, I guess I told him the truth."

"And what was that?"

I ran a hand absently through my hair, wishing to be anywhere but withering beneath the doctor's gaze.

"I told him I was lonely, that I needed a friend."

"And did you find one?"

I smiled, the first relaxed thing I'd done since André had snuck up on us.

"Most definitely."

I grabbed my backpack, stood, and slung it over my shoulder. "I'd better get going. The bus took forever, and I have no idea what the return will look like at this hour."

"You rode the bus?" André looked like he might faint. The French were expressive, indeed.

I nodded. "I didn't need a car in Nashville. Guess I'll have to go shopping sometime soon."

André's expression didn't relax. "You took a bus for nearly two hours to visit a boy you knew wasn't speaking to anyone?"

"He spoke to me."

André scoffed. "He gave you his name."

"That's more than he's given anyone in ... how long?"

"Five weeks."

"Five weeks. There you have it. He'd spoken to me, and I wanted to learn more, to hear more from him. So yeah, I took a long-ass bus ride to see him."

André stared, and I knew the psychiatrist part of his brain was working overtime. I half expected him to invite me into his office so I could lie on his couch and be dissected. I did not expect the invitation he offered.

"Would you like to have dinner with me? I could drive you home afterward. You would arrive at the same time as if you had taken the bus."

"The bus" came out "*ze* bus" and I nearly laughed. Then I realized he was serious.

And staring.

And his eyes were ... damn, I hadn't noticed how blue they were, with tiny flecks of green when he smiled. I wanted to reach up and take his thick black-rimmed glasses off so I could see those eyes without their shields, see if they brightened or retreated.

"Um, okay. Sure, I guess," I said.

He snorted. "I appreciate your enthusiasm. It has been a long time since I asked anyone for a date."

Holy shit. Had I heard him right? Had he just called us going to dinner a *date*? I tried to remember if anyone had told me Doc was gay, but his uptight, nose-in-the-air attitude had turned me off so badly before that it hadn't registered.

His nose wasn't in the air now. In fact, it was perfectly positioned above a pair of slightly moist lips that curled at the corners. I didn't mean to stare at his lips. They were just lips. But dammit. They were perky, kissable, lickable lips ... and he was French. He would know *ze* French kiss, right? God, I wanted *ze* French kiss.

"Sorry, yeah, I'd like that. A date with a doc. Sounds nice."

His smile shifted from placating professional to a level of warmth and depth I hadn't known he'd possessed. Something in my chest did a backflip, and I nearly banged my knee against a chair walking behind him ... watching him walk ... watching his behind as we walked.

Damn, he had a nice behind.

Twelve

ANDRÉ

"Any thoughts on where you would like to eat?" I asked as we drove up I-71 toward the heart of Columbus.

Nick's only suggestion thus far had been to eat somewhere near his apartment so I didn't have to drive too far out of my way. His apartment was well out of my way, since I lived across the street from the Ranch, but I didn't say that. It was refreshingly adorable that he expressed concern for my convenience when he had taken a two-hour bus ride to visit one of my patients. Set aside how handsome he was ... and athletic ... and how dreamy his smile was when the skin around his eyes crinkled ... yes, set all that aside. More important than his damnable dimples, he continued to surprise in how conscientious and thoughtful he was, not at all the stuck-on-his-own-greatness baseball player I'd pegged him for after our first encounter.

"I'm new to town, remember? Outside of the first night when the guys took me to a brewpub near the stadium, I've either eaten at home or on the road with the team for the past week. At this point, Denny's sounds like fine dining."

I nearly ran the car off the road. "*Merde*, Nick, no. Just no. There will be no Denny's for dinner tonight, not on our first date."

He grinned as I said "first date."

"Do you trust me?" I asked.

He turned toward me. "No offense, but I don't know you."

"That's fair. But I am French, and we are talking about food. You can trust me."

He chuckled. "When you put it that way ..."

"Excellent! Rodizio it is."

"Rodizio? That doesn't sound French."

"It's not, but it's *magnifique*. You will love it."

The evening crowd had thinned as we strolled into Rodizio Brazilian Steakhouse, and we were seated without a wait. I watched with pleasure as Nick's eyes widened with each buffet bar we passed. When three waiters whizzed by with huge chunks of meat on long metal skewers, I thought he might drool.

"Doc, you didn't need to bring me somewhere fancy."

I grinned. "That's the second time in two days I have been accused of being fancy. Not all French are fancy, Nick."

He looked confused, but held his tongue.

Once we were seated, the waiter explained the red- and green-sided coasters. Green meant we were open to being served more meat. Red was a stop sign. Nick lusted over the passing meats like a horny teenager flipping through his first *Penthouse*. I doubted his card would ever turn red.

"What would you like to drink?" the server asked.

Nick hesitated, so I cleared my throat. "Do you mind if I choose?"

"No, go ahead." He motioned with an open palm.

"A bottle of Cabernet, the 2008 BR Cohn Silver Label, please."

"Right away, sir. Help yourselves to the buffet." The server gave a polite dip of his head and vanished to retrieve our wine.

"This is all so nice," Nick said. "They barely pay us in the minors, so eating like this is a real treat."

"Really? I thought all pro players—"

He actually laughed. "Everyone thinks that. If I make it to the majors, then we can talk money. Until then, I'm more of a poor college student than professional sportsman."

Nick Dunlap continued evolving before my eyes. With each layer peeled back, I sensed a dozen more. For one steeped in examining people, understanding them, Nick was quickly becoming a fascination.

And then he batted his eyes like a teenager and flicked an unruly curl off his forehead, and I nearly swooned my ass off my chair right there in the middle of the restaurant.

"Let's hit the buffet. They're going to lose money on me tonight," he said with a toothy grin, grabbing his plate and practically running from the table without checking to see if I was behind him.

His boyish enthusiasm was infectious, and I suddenly realized who he reminded me of.

A certain boy who only recently began speaking again.

Nick had left his cell phone on the table, so I decided to wait until he returned to forage for salad and sides. A grin spread as I watched him bounce from one bar to the next. The lighting in the restaurant was mostly dim, but bright lights lit each stage of food. As Nick drifted in and out of those lights, I got a better look at the man I'd invited to dinner.

He really was beautiful; not the classically chiseled, perfect piece of man-meat one might drool over on the cover of certain magazines found on the top row of the grocery store or gas station—not that I had ever drooled over those pages ... much. No, Nick was adorably handsome, with boyish features just awakening to manhood, and thick wavy hair that rebelled nearly as often as it fell into place. It wasn't exactly curly, more messy, but several locks in the front curled as if they'd spent time in a hot iron and wriggled their way across his forehead. I'd lost count of how many times he'd shoved the trouble-some locks out of the way.

He was fit, but not overly so. His neck did not bulge, and there were no arteries or veins forming a nationwide interstate map across his arms. Although his arms *were* corded and thick, causing the banding of his shirt to strain every time he lifted anything.

That almost made me break out into a sweat.

But it wasn't even his looks that had me contorted more than a player in a Cirque show. It was him, his personality, his demeanor, the way his every word and action surprised me and went against all of my initial assumptions. I was a professional in the people-reading vocation. Leaping to conclusions was a cardinal sin in my line of work. And yet, I had done just that when I'd met Nick a week ago. I was so sure he was a pretty-boy jock who only cared about fast cars and quick lays, that I'd completely ignored all the signals he was sending, conscious and otherwise, that spoke to a quiet confidence—and lack of confidence—that was utterly endearing.

I found myself more curious with every answer, more desirous of the next question. And yet, he was twenty years my junior. The psychiatrist alarms in my head were blaring warnings louder than London's air-raid sirens during the war. It wasn't that guys with distant birthdates couldn't make things work, it's that they rarely did. An age gap might be a thrilling trope for a storybook romance, but they crashed and burned more times than they flew anywhere in real life.

Nick could be Adonis himself, descended from wherever they made such men, and the odds would still be stacked so far against us, so far against *me* ... The last thing I needed was another crash and burn.

"They have this noodle salad thing on that third table. Oh god, I think I jizzed." Nick flopped down beside me, thunking down two plates whose towering contents teetered as they came to rest. "Shit, I probably shouldn't say jizzed. You'll think ... crap ... sorry. Guess I'm a little excited about all this food ... and maybe a little nervous."

My lips curled again. "Nervous? Really?"

He glared at his pasta salad, then slowly glanced up. "Yeah. It's been a while since ... you know."

I raised a questioning brow. "I do not know. Tell me."

"Why don't you get your food before the meat boys start showing up?"

I snorted at "meat boys" and the image that conjured.

"Good idea. You left your phone, so I wanted to wait. The server should be here with our wine soon. Please don't wait to start."

Nick's cheek was already pooched out like a squirrel hoarding nuts. He stopped chewing long enough to give me a guilty look, which only made me laugh again.

"Enjoy, Nick. I like seeing you happy."

Why did I say that? I thought as I lumbered away from the table, sure he was thinking I was some lecherous old man trying to steal his soul. Gah! Dating was a minefield, and I lost my feet a very long time ago.

I returned a short time later to find Nick had cleaned both plates and was sipping wine.

"This wine is amazing." He raised his glass toward me.

I sat and set my half-filled plate on the table.

"Are you not hungry?" he asked.

I snorted. "This is a normal plate for us non-athletes. You eat your fill and don't worry about me."

He shrugged. "You don't have to tell me twice."

And up he went to fill new plates with more delicacies.

I stabbed a roasted cherry tomato and marveled at the clean-picked-bones of plates stacked before his chair.

He returned as the first of the "meat boys" arrived with what looked like an entire cow on a spear.

"Prime rib?" he asked.

"God, yes." Nick didn't wait for me to reply, just stabbed his plate toward the beef bearer.

"Did Ethan tell you anything else interesting? Anything we didn't discuss earlier?"

His expression sobered and his fork froze halfway to his mouth. After a pause, he set the uneaten bite down and said, "Back to business?"

I raised a palm. "Forgive me. I didn't mean to ruin a wonderful evening. It's just ... do you know how remarkable it is that Ethan spoke with you, that he allowed you to hold him like that?"

Nick cocked his head. "I guess I don't. He acted like a normal boy. At least, that's what I saw."

I took a fortifying sip of wine, then set my glass down and steepled my fingers.

"Nick, I have been working with children for twenty years. Never before has a child simply turned off, as Sara likes to say. I have seen children go quiet after a trauma or triggering event, but there was nothing with Ethan, nothing we have identified. He simply flipped off."

I grabbed my fork and absently moved a piece of potato around my plate, ordering my thoughts.

"Nick, Sara and I have tried so many things. Ethan has had more sessions in the past month than he has had in years. Nothing worked. He wouldn't budge. He was never unpleasant, but he refused to speak, and most of the time, he simply stared out the window as we asked him questions or spoke. In one visit, all that changed."

"That's a little dramatic. All he did was give me his name. He didn't say anything else."

I waved a hand in the air. "That's just it, Nick, it *is* that dramatic. One word can be a breakthrough that opens a mind. By getting one word, you unlocked Ethan's mind and touched his heart."

Nick leaned back and began fidgeting with his fingers. I knew I was making him uncomfortable, but I couldn't stop myself.

"Then you came back, on your own, and the boy embraced you, figuratively and literally. Emotionally speaking, he is reaching out to you. Do you not see how wonderful this is?"

Nick stared into the distance, and for the first time that night, I knew he wasn't ogling the buffet.

"He's a sweet boy."

Now it was my turn to sit back. Again, Nick had surprised me, in the best possible way.

Then he asked, "How long has he been at the Ranch? He made it seem like his whole childhood."

I sighed. "It has been many years. His parents died when he was four, a double overdose the police suspect was a suicide. He was lucky they didn't choose to take him with them."

"Dear god."

"When he came to us, he expressed all the classic symptoms associated with a child born of an addict: stunted growth, hyperactivity, extreme anxiety resulting in sleep deprivation, and a host of other symptoms. The poor little man was a mess, and he was unadoptable. Our best foster parents who specialize in medically challenged children couldn't handle his psychological needs, so we kept him here. Before we knew it, one year had turned into four."

Nick's expression carried disbelief mingled with grief. "He said he doesn't have many friends, that they leave too often, either through adoption or placement. He said he's afraid to make friends because he knows he'll lose them."

I nodded slowly. "He's coping the best way he knows how. It's remarkable a child his age can put all of that into words. Usually, they internalize it but struggle to explain what they're feeling. We have to use art or other tools to understand what they're thinking. As stunted as his physical growth may be, he is mature beyond his years."

Two more meat boys arrived. Then another, then another. Chicken, pork, lamb, octopus, and two different fishes were presented. Nick, claiming it would be rude not to try each one, devoured everything set—or stabbed—before him.

If I had been surprised before, I was flabbergasted now.

He couldn't simply eat. He could eat it all.

"There was another boy there last week, an older one. Fifteen, maybe sixteen, longish dark hair. Looked like he was mad at the world and very alone. He sat in the back by himself."

"That would be Noah."

"What's his story? I mean, what you can tell me. I get it if you can't say much."

My grin was tight. How could I explain Noah?

"Noah has been with us longer than any other child. Except for two stints as a guest of the juvenile penal system, he has lived with us for more than thirteen years."

Nick whistled.

"He's a tough case. Some people were never born with a fair chance. I believe Noah is one of them."

Nick straightened. "Sounds like you've given up on him."

"No, no. Please, I would never give up on anyone, especially a child, but Noah ... how do I say ... he is in the rebellious stage. This would be challenging for any parent, a sixteen-year-old boy who wants to show out, but Noah lacks much of the foundation children normally receive in a loving home. He has never known stability beyond the walls and fences of the Ranch, and a few of us who have been there with him."

I dabbed my lips with a cloth napkin, more to buy time than anything. "Nick, as much as we try to help, we are not parents. We cannot *be* parents, not to him or any child there. We are their doctors, sometimes their friends, but that is as close as our relationship can be for our objectivity and professional judgment to remain strong. That limits the guidance we can offer, the emotional development a child can experience through us."

Nick crossed his arms. "Ethan needed to be held."

I stared, open-mouthed, speechless.

"Ethan needed someone to care for him enough to open their arms and hold him, to let him squeeze and nuzzle and feel cared for. He needed to be a child and to be loved. I understand therapy better than you might think." His voice lowered. "I get it, but sometimes what a child needs is healing of the heart, not the head."

As our server arrived to refill our glasses, I wondered at the wisdom coming from this professional baseball player regarding children I'd cared for all their lives. I wondered how I'd missed his simple truth, the obvious understanding of needs and desires that went beyond any textbook or test, any medicine or exercise. I wondered—

"I would like to come back, to see Ethan again. Would that be alright?"

I took a sip of my now-full glass, spilling a bit on the napkin in my lap.

"Ugh, I am clumsy," I said, dabbing where a drop had fallen on my shirt. "Nick, I think that would be wonderful. He owes you a lesson in grounders, no?"

Nick's smile shone brighter than the buffet lamps. "That he does."

Conversation veered to less serious territory. Nick asked about the best cheap places to eat in town, so I gave him a virtual tour, occasionally whipping out my phone to show him street-facing views of buildings or restaurants.

Somehow, after consuming a small nation's worth of meat and vegetables, Nick managed to down three different desserts. When he insisted I take at least one bite of each, I was sure my slacks would burst open, but he'd been right, the mango concoction was delicious.

"Marcus would love this place," he said absently as he swirled the last few sips of wine left in his glass. I was feeling a bit light-headed, and he'd had two glasses more than me. The glassy sheen in his eyes told me he was about to be either sleepy or really funny.

"Marcus?"

"My roommate. He was with us at the Ranch last week. Big, tan, perfect-looking guy. I mean, *model-perfect* asshole. He's from Brazil. This place is Brazilian, right?"

I nodded. "It is. And I remember him. He is rather, well—"

"He's *fucking* hot. You can say it. And he's nice and funny ... and a lot smarter that you'd think, you know, being all swarthy and sexy. He's also my *straight* roommate, which makes him unattainably, untouchably, unlickably annoying."

I grunted a half-tipsy laugh. "Is someone crushing on his roomie?"

"No. I mean, I would, but he's straight, and I don't need a toaster."

My brow furrowed. "A toaster?"

"Dear Jesus, not you too. Does no one teach you gays anything?"

I giggled. "I have not been teachable for a very long time, my young friend."

"Young?" He cocked a brow. "Are you going to play the 'I have gray hair and am twenty years older than you' card? Is that how this goes?"

"*Quoi*—"

"Oh, don't go all French on me now," he slurred merrily. "If I kiss you later, are you going to have senior guilt because I'm so much younger than you?"

"Senior? Who said I was a senior?"

He smirked and downed the last of his wine.

"I am older than you, but fortysomething isn't senior!"

"It's senior to me ... by, like, a lot. A whole lot."

"Wait." I finished my wine and tried to hold it up like a stop sign, then set it down. "Did you say something about kissing me?"

"See! Hard of hearing. Forgetful. Definitely senior."

"I may have to teach you respect."

His grin turned into a glower. "Maybe I'd like that."

Thirteen

ANDRÉ

The next morning, I sat in my office, sipping steaming tea and staring out the window, waiting for my PC to finish whirring and beeping through its startup routine. The Ranch was on the cutting edge of treatment and therapy, but was so far behind in technology, one might've thought the Atari 2600 hooked to the television in the game room was a new release. My computer wasn't far from that vintage, and, unlike certain wines, computers did not become better—or faster—with age.

A pair of neighborhood cats scurried by. No one knew where they slept at night, but most of their meals consisted of freshly browned ground beef with leftover veggies, furnished courtesy of our kitchen staff, served on white porcelain plates set just outside the back door. The pair was inseparable. Mollie was covered in thick, lustrous black fur, while Max sported a frizzy brown coat that shot in every direction. On their stroll past my window, Max leaned into his mate and nuzzled her neck.

"Aww. You go Max. Show her who loves her," I muttered over my mug.

"Feeling romantic this morning?"

I nearly tossed my tea across the office at the sound of Sara's voice.

"Dear god, Sara, could you please make some noise when you enter? You almost had to call the paramedics for my heart just then."

"You're *so* dramatic. You know that, right?" She smirked as she plopped into one of the leather chairs opposite my desk. "You ready for this morning?"

I checked my light blue dress shirt for signs of tea damage, then sat. "What am I ready for? I would look at my schedule, but this computer was found after the attack on the Bastille and will take another century to start up."

She rolled her eyes. "I don't even know what that means, but I'll assume you're being dramatic again. You gays are all alike."

My brow rose. "Is that a fact? Is our beloved doctor of psychiatry stereotyping my people? Should I wave a flag or start a chant in protest? Toss some glitter or chiffon?"

She snorted. "I'd pay good money to see you covered in glitter and chiffon."

"I'll have you know, I almost had my gay card revoked last night over a toaster."

Her expression turned blank. "A toaster?"

"*Exactement*!"

Her blank stare lingered, but I refused to be her LGBT educator. Toasters be damned.

"So, what am I to be ready for this morning?"

She straightened in her chair. "For Ethan. You have a session with him in"—she checked her watch—"fifteen minutes."

"Oh, right. It is Thursday, isn't it?"

She nodded. "I figured after the breakthrough with that baseball player last night, you would be excited for this session."

My chair groaned as I leaned back, tapping my fingertips together. "That was ... something."

She cocked her head. "André Luis Adolfo Martin the Third, what are you hiding from me?"

"*Quoi*?" I raised both brows innocently.

"There. That's two tells. First, you tapped your fingertips, which you only do when you're remembering something—not when you're pondering, when you're remembering. Second, you did that thing with your eyebrows you always claim is just a French expression, although you never said what it expresses. I think it says, 'I'm fucking hiding something from my best friend.' Now, out with it before I do more than make you spill tea all over your prissy little ass."

"*Allons*! My ass is not ... prissy."

"It most certainly is. Now talk. We only have a few minutes left."

I folded my hands in my lap, careful not to tap, steeple, stroke, or anything else that might give Dr. Psychic more ammunition.

"Nick and I—"

"Nick? The baseball player you swore was stuck on himself? The one who may have helped us—"

"*Oui*. That Nick."

She scooched up to the edge of her chair and leaned forward. "Go on."

I blew out a breath. "He took the bus here yesterday."

She waited, then shrugged. "So?"

"It was a two-hour trip—one way."

"Still not seeing a connection. Why do we care?"

"Well, because I may have felt sorry for him having to take the long ride home. I might have offered to drive him home, but with one condition."

Her fingers began dancing on my desk. "Okay? And that condition was?"

"That he let me buy him dinner, on a date, before dropping him off at his home."

"Did you call it a date, or did you, in your vague French way, insinuate dinner is always a date and he should simply know your mind and heart when he dines in your presence?"

I tried not to laugh, but Sara was ridiculous and funny.

"I called it a date. He even ... how do the kids say it? He busted me on it. Asked if I had just asked him out on a date."

"Oh, wow. That's wonderful, André! How did it go? Where did you take him? Did you get to see his bat and balls?"

"Sara!"

"I'm assuming we'll have to use baseball references now. Did you get to first? And what does that mean to you? That wasn't a psych question about your feelings. I want a literal definition like I might find in a textbook. Draw me a picture if you must. Actually, I like pictures. Definitely draw me a picture."

"Sara—""Unless you took a picture or had a hidden video camera … maybe he's into that. I would totally watch you two—"

"Sara! There was no picture taking or movie making or ball touching."

"What about his bat?"

"No! No bat!"

"Geez. So hostile. And a little chicken shit. I would've gone for the bat."

I threw back into my headrest and begged the ceiling to fall on me, or for the earth to open up, or for anything to disrupt this inane conversation.

"Uh, Doc?"

Both our heads whipped up at the sound of a small voice, almost a whisper, coming from my woefully open office door.

"Ethan. Thank goodness. You just saved me from … well … you saved me. Dr. Adams was just leaving. Very quietly. She was leaving very quietly without saying a word about sports or sporting equipment."

Sara burst out laughing, hopped out of her chair, and strolled past Ethan, mussing his hair on her way out. "You boys have a good talk. Nice to see you, Ethan."

"You too," the confused lad said.

I stared a moment, realizing Ethan had just spoken more words to the two of us in a matter of moments than he had in months. My heart lifted—and my pulse quickened.

"Come in, have a seat over on the couch. I'll come around. No need to be formal today."

"Um, okay," he said, looking sideways at me as he wove his way around the coffee table to the couch.

I snatched a notepad and pen off my desk, glanced sadly into the nearly empty mug, then made my way to sit in a chair on the foot-end of the couch, assuming my patient was lying down, which Ethan was not.

My clinical brain was going into overdrive.

"How was your visit with the baseball player yesterday? What was his name?"

I knew perfectly well what Nick Dunlap's name was. It was all I had thought about all morning. His stupid eyes and dimples were all I could see every time I closed my eyes. Oh, and that curl that kept flopping down. I'd pushed that thing back a hundred times since waking with the broadest smile this morning.

Yes, I knew his name, but I wanted to keep Ethan talking.

"Nick," he said.

"Oh, right. I knew it was something like that. How was your chat with Nick? It looked like you had a nice visit."

He hesitated, then nodded, and a hint of a smile crept across his face. "Dr. André, he's so cool."

I found myself smiling. He was.

"How so?"

"He came down here just to see me yesterday. Did you know that?"

I did. "That's wonderful."

"He really wanted to see me. At first, I thought maybe ..." His eyes drifted to the floor.

"You thought what?"

"Maybe you ... or Dr. Sara ... maybe you put him up to visiting."

I shook my head. "Ethan, if we thought it would help you, we would arrange a visit with almost anyone, but we didn't have anything to do with Nick coming to see you yesterday."

"I know! He told me that too." He lit back up. "And he gave me his homer ball ... and a new glove signed by all the players. Coach even signed it. It's so cool. Is it bad that I slept with it on my hand last night?"

"No, you sleep with that glove anytime you like." I had to stifle a laugh. "What did you two talk about?"

His tiny shoulders rose, then fell. "I don't know. Nothing, really. I asked him about baseball and playing on a team and all. He asked me about living here."

That was a surprise. "Really? What did he ask about?"

"Just if I liked it. How long I'd been here. That sort of thing."

"How did it make you feel when he asked those things?"

The pause that followed that question made me wonder if I'd just silenced him all over again, and I found myself holding my breath.

He finally spoke. "Sad."

I breathed. "Why sad?"

"I don't know." He started picking at a fingernail, then turning his hands over and examining them. "It made me remember stuff."

I scribbled a note and waited.

He didn't continue.

"What stuff?"

"My old friends, mostly. They've all left." He lifted his legs and sat atop his feet, then leaned against the arm rest with his head laying on it like a pillow. I almost had to lean in to hear him when he spoke. "I think I saw my mom too."

I leaned in. "Your mom? You saw her?"

"Yeah. In my mind. At least, I think it was her. I don't remember what she looked like so good anymore."

I had to swallow hard.

I was trained to be clinical, to not share my emotions with my patients, but this boy ..."Was seeing your mom what made you sad?"

He nodded against the leather. "And my friends. I miss them."

"I bet you do. That's normal, Ethan, to miss people, to be sad, even. It's okay to feel those things."

"Maybe. It still sucks.""Yeah, it does."

Without lifting his head, his eyes met mine, and my heart ached with the pain that filled them. "Dr. André, there's always new kids, and ... I know I should make new friends. It just, it feels like ... like it's dumb to even try. They're just going to leave."

"Nick came back."

I had no idea where that came from, and I knew the moment it left my mouth I shouldn't have said it. I didn't know Nick Dunlap. He could vanish and add to this boy's stack of missing persons. Using his presence was a terrible thing, yet I had just done exactly that—and there were no take-backs in therapy.

Ethan sat up and wiped his eyes and turned to me with hope pouring from his tiny frame. The words he then echoed pierced my soul.

"Nick came back."

Fourteen

Nick

I woke that morning unusually wide awake and chipper, and neither of those things described me in the morning—ever.

In an effort to save my nickels, I hadn't joined a local gym, opting to take a bus back to the stadium where our team's weight room welcomed me home. I'd taken a few days off after the end of our season, and the soreness of a "first workout" felt good, like I was pushing my body to a new level all over again, even though I knew it was more akin to knocking off the dust that had settled over a period of laziness.

After an hour of weights, burning the shit out of my chest and biceps, I hopped on the treadmill and jogged at a comfortable pace for thirty minutes. Outfielders stood for long periods, then sprinted, but, despite my sunny disposition that morning, I didn't feel up to the machine's maniacal interval training setting. That bitch hurt.

Sweat dripped from my brow and arms as I stepped off the belt. Wobbly legs reminded me how brutal it was to get back into a routine after a few days away. I promised myself to make the best use of my off-season, to work out every day, eat right, and barge through the spring training door ready for action.

It was five months and several holidays away.

That was a hollow promise, but I was proud of myself for try-ing—well, thinking about trying—even if I knew the trying would take significant breaks in between efforts.

Rationalization complete, I hobbled into the empty locker room, stripped down, and showered. It was strange to be here, in the heart of the team's shrine, with none of my new brothers around. It felt even stranger to not hear Marcus and his silky accent making some errant remark in his not-quite-English. I missed the big guy, and that surprised me.

As I toweled off, his locker caught my eye. He'd stuck a Brazilian flag magnet over the school-hallway-style number, which made me think of a dozen pranks I should play on him when he came back into town in the new year. It also made me wish he'd be around for the holidays. I wouldn't be traveling. I didn't have anywhere to go or anyone to see. Holidays were just a reminder of things I didn't have ... anymore.

Memories of parents who were there, then gone, made me think of Ethan and all the poor boy had suffered in his short life. Somehow, he still smiled. He clearly struggled with his past—and present—but when given a chance, and the right motivation, he saw past his sadness.

I'd helped him do that. I'd made him smile.

Still, my heart was heavy for us both, for all we'd lost, for all we'd never know. We were alike in so many ways. I knew that should be encouraging, make me feel like I wasn't alone, but it didn't. It just made me more sad that he would have to cope with all the things I carried around each day, all the demons I'd faced—all the ones I still faced when my eyes closed at night and darkness folded around me.

And with that, I draped a literal—and figurative—wet towel over my post-pump mood.

"Dude, stop that shit. The past is the past. You've risen above all that. You're on your way to the majors. You're on an amazing team, even if they didn't make playoffs this year. You've got the best roomie ever, despite his fucked-up straightness. Life is good. Stop being an idiot."

Chiding myself never really worked, but there was no one else in the locker room to do it, so I manned up and gave myself a good scolding. The mental image of me wagging a finger at myself made me chuckle.

"Great. Now you're cracking up, going completely insane. Who laughs at themselves while standing naked in a locker room with a towel on their head? Dude, really?"

And yes, I was carrying on a full, out-loud conversation with myself, naked in the middle of the locker room, while staring at a Brazilian flag magnet and drying my hair with a soaked-through towel that only spread the wetness rather than dried it.

That made me laugh harder.

Before I realized it, I was on the floor, laughing so hard tears streamed down my face.

Moments later, when the laughter and tears finally faded, I sat on the floor with my back to the wooden bench, staring without seeing the lockers across the room. Images of Ethan swirled through my mind. When I'd handed him the baseball, it was like someone had flipped a light switch and the whole world blazed with warmth. Then, when he saw the glove and all the signatures and he threw himself into my arms, my heart almost shattered into a million pieces.

What was it about the happiness of a child? Why did it make one's heart sing? How could a tiny laugh make one feel like everything was perfect and wonderful in that single, frozen moment of time?

I'd never had much experience with kids. Other than teammates, I'd never been around kids much, even as a kid myself, and certainly not as an adult. They were a mystery to me, and whatever had happened with Ethan only added to my perplexity.

But I knew one thing: I wanted to see him again, to see if he would keep talking, keep smiling, keep asking me to return.

I could see his short, straight hair frizzing around his ears and falling across his forehead. His quirky grin was so clear in my mind. And the sound of his laugh. God, could there be a better sound? I suddenly had the urge to tickle him, to make him giggle uncontrollably, to hear that sound and imprint it on my mind.

On my heart.

Then, in my daydream's eye, I looked up to find André staring down, smiling, his eyes twinkling as I tortured his charge into another glee-filled fit.

André.

He was an enigma.

Half the time, he looked at me like I was some kind of zoo animal who belonged back in his cage, far away from normal folk, even farther from him. Just when I thought getting to know him was a mistake, he'd say something sweet or funny in that sexy French accent and my heart would tremble.

I'd never dated much. Baseball had always been my life, and falling in love was a complication no aspiring pro athlete needed. Success required focus—extreme focus. Men were a distraction.

My mental meandering was clear evidence of that.

I was distracted ... by André.

And it felt like a warm blanket wrapping around my shoulders on a wintry morning.

Shit. I hated how good it felt, how good thinking about him felt, how good I was sure his arms around me would feel.

My heart longed to feel that comfort, yet I knew I couldn't afford to go there. I had to rein this in—whatever *this* was.

Besides, *this* wouldn't last. He'd get to know me, then he'd run. The good ones always did.

Hell, anyone close to me did. It was the story of my life outside of baseball.

And there it was, the simple truth I knew in the depths of my soul: the sport was my one constant, my rock, my tether to normalcy that never abandoned me.

It was the one thing that was true.

If I worked hard and committed—*really* committed—myself, baseball was a loyal mistress ... mister ... master?

I wasn't sure how that worked for a dude who liked dudes.

Anyway.

Baseball was loyal. It could be cruel sometimes, but it never left. It never drifted away in the night or vanished when I wasn't paying attention. It never promised to be there, then wasn't, when I needed it most. Baseball was steady. It was stable. It gave me purpose.

I would never leave it. Not for anyone.

I closed my eyes to see the diamond, to relive memories of games, of victories, of triumphs. I wanted to revel in the feel of the glove on my hand, the ball in my palm, the clay of the infield and grass near the track. I wanted to be one with my love.

But brains are funny things. I didn't see a baseball or a diamond.

When I squeezed my eyes shut, I saw a man.

André's wavy hair, gray streaks flowing in the breeze, appeared in my mind. We were so close, my face inches from his, exploring, teasing, roaming. I could smell the sweetness of his cologne, just a hint, enough to make me want to bury my nose in his neck and inhale his essence ...

Dammit. No.

I would not go there. I couldn't.

His smile was more alluring than his scent. Warm and inviting. Honest and pure. The warmth of a crackling fire and the heat of a blue flame. I wanted to feel those lips against my own, to taste them, to run my tongue and teeth over—

Fuck me. This had to stop.

I tossed my towel into the empty hamper and changed into clean clothes, stuffing my dirties into a plastic bag before cramming them into my backpack. The bus passed near the stadium every twelve minutes, which gave me exactly four minutes to get to the bus stop.

With seconds to spare, I skidded before the bench and watched the bus round the corner.

Four stops later, I hopped off and destroyed two Nacho Bell Grandes and six soft tacos. The kids behind the counter laughed when I told them it was all for me, then gaped as I tossed back the last bite and refilled my tea for the third time. I guess they hadn't seen many pro athletes darken their door.

Fully stuffed, I waddled back to the street and waited for the next bus to arrive. My plan was to go home, do some laundry, walk to the nearby grocery store and stock up, then cook a quiet dinner and watch reruns of *$100,000 Pyramid*. I loved the bonus round, especially if Rosie O'Donnell was on the show. She was brilliant, exactly the woman I wanted at my dinner party on game night. She'd be a vicious opponent, just what my dear ole teammates deserved.

That made me grin.

I settled back into my seat and let my mind drift ...

The bus lurched to a stop, jarring me awake. I rubbed my eyes, glanced out the window, and realized I'd done something truly stupid.

If anyone was born without a sense of direction, it was me. I could get lost pulling out of my own driveway. If it wasn't so funny, it would be embarrassing.

Not only had I fallen asleep, but the bus was also headed south instead of north toward my apartment. I'd boarded the right route, just on the wrong side of the street. Who does that?

"You are such an idiot," I said, chuckling to myself.

A quick glance at my phone told me I'd been on the darn thing for more than an hour.

I looked around, trying to get my bearings as we began moving again. Going by the streets I vaguely recognized, and my blurry math, we were a few stops from the Ranch. Had my subconscious mind tricked me into making another trek to see Ethan ... or his doctor?

Frustration over my groggy error was replaced by a thrill as I thought of seeing him, though I wasn't sure which *him* I was more thrilled to see.

Would they even let me see Ethan without an appointment?

I knew they had visiting hours, but those were supposed to be for relatives. Would their graciousness to a player extend another day? I had helped them with a troubled boy, after all.

Maybe I could say I was there to see André instead. There couldn't be a prohibition for visitors seeing the staff, could there?

That was a terrible idea.

He'd think I was stalking him at his work, showing up out of the blue. We'd had a nice time—a really nice time—but he hadn't so much as pecked my cheek when I got out of the car. That meant he wasn't into me, didn't it? He was French. They kissed pretty much anyone, anytime. They kissed to say "hello" or "go fuck yourself."

If he was actually interested and just being all mature, whatever that was worth, I might be blowing any chance I had with him by showing up on his doorstep. He would think I was some desperate, lost puppy who had nowhere to be and no one to love and ...

Okay, so I *was* that puppy, but he didn't need to know that.

Hell. The bus jarred to a stop. To *the* stop.

This was the Ranch's stop.

Crap. Crap, crap, crap, crap.

The doors opened, and the driver craned her head back toward me. "Hon, this is you, isn't it?"

Great, even the bus driver knew I was here for ...

What was I here for?

I made my way toward the front, thanked the driver, and stepped off.

Fifteen

Nick

"Nick!" an excited, high-pitched voice screamed from across the grassy yard.

I'd been standing at the gate for several minutes, waiting for the voice I hadn't recognized to check with a higher power for approval of my unscheduled visit. After a brief internal debate, I'd stated I was there to see Ethan again. I wasn't sure if André was out at work, or if he would be bothered by an admirer suddenly showing up at his professional doorstep, so I opted for a visit with a patient. It seemed the safer route.

"Hey buddy," I said as Ethan slammed into the iron fence, gripping my fingers like they were the last fries in his Happy Meal.

His smile made my heart soar. "I didn't know you were coming again today. Can we do that lesson?"

I grinned. "That's why I'm here. It's the off-season, so all my coaches are away. I need you to keep me in playing shape."

I hadn't thought it was possible for his smile to widen, but it nearly reached his ears at that.

"You bet. I'm a good coach."

I chuckled. "I bet you are."

Buzz.

"Come on in, Mr. Dunlap. One of our staff will find Ethan for you," the voice, now friendlier, said through the speaker.

"He's right here. The little monster saw me standing at the gate."

"Oh, you're not in a car?"

"No, I took the bus again," I said, leaving out the accidental part of that statement.

"Alright. Let us know if you need anything. There should be staff around the yard."

"Thank you," I said, striding through the now-open gate.

Ethan slammed into me, his tiny arms gripping my waist. I knelt down and lifted him so his arms were around my neck, so I could hug him back.

"Good to see you too, bud."

I wouldn't have taken this eight-year-old for a giggler, but the sound made me grin so big it hurt. Without thinking, I reached down and dug my fingers into his ribs. The quiet giggling morphed into full-throated wails of tortured delight as he dropped to the ground. I fell to my knees beside him and redoubled my attack. His feet failed and tears streaked his face. My own laughter rose to match his innocent glee in a most beautiful harmony.

"Oh, great. He's back, and he's tormenting our children."

A distinctly French cadence added to our song.

I looked up but continued poking and prodding. "Hey, Doc. Miss me yet?"

He smirked, and one bushy brow rose. "You presume much, Mr. Toaster."

I barked a laugh at that, then released my victim so I could stand. "We discussed this, my dear doctor. I have no need of a toaster. I don't want one. I don't even like toast."

"Everybody likes toast," Ethan piped in, an utterly baffled expression on his face.

André and I burst out laughing.

"What? What's so funny?" Ethan demanded. "You're weird if you don't like toast."

I gripped him under his armpits and tossed him in the air like he weighed nothing—which was close to the truth for the undersized boy. "I am weird, but you like me anyway."

He giggled again as I tossed him higher.

"No way!" he screamed.

"Yes way!" I roared back.

"I see you two are having a deep and meaningful conversation, so I will leave you to it. I just wanted to say hello." André offered a slight tilt of his head, then turned to head toward the building.

"Doc." My voice stilled him. "Mind if we catch up after my visit with this little rugrat? I have ... a few questions for you."

His brow did that thing again. "Questions? For me?"

"Yeah, about something, um, we discussed last night."

His other brow shot up, then he glanced at his watch.

"It's three thirty now. I should be done with my day around four forty-five or so. Meet me in the common room, the place you first visited?" He pointed toward the building nearest where we stood.

I nodded. "Sure. See you then."

"*Avec plaisir*," he said, then strode away.

"What does 'avac plastic' mean?" Ethan asked, failing to sound out his French syllables, but doing about as well as I would have.

"I have no idea, bud. I'll add that to my list of questions for Doc." I pulled my backpack off my shoulder. "I think, somewhere in here, I have my glove. Do you still have yours?"

"Duh! It's in my room. I'll go get it."

Before I could speak, he streaked across the yard and into the building. I ambled across the grass toward the playground to sit on a nearby bench and wait. Despite the stunning sunshine, there was a nip in the air, and only a few kids played nearby. The sounds of their chatter and laughter kept me company while I waited.

Ethan and I played catch for over an hour. He took his role as my fielding coach very seriously, hurling the ball as fast as his underdeveloped arm would allow, making it bounce and turn against the grassy ground. The glove I'd brought him was made for a boy his age, but I hadn't taken into consideration how much smaller he was than a typical eight-year-old, and he struggled to keep it on every time he reached for the ball.

"Ethan!" a woman's voice called around four thirty. I looked up as he turned to see a woman whose graying hair had been tightly spun into a bun. My juvenile brain wanted to run and hug her, shouting an Opie-esque "Aunt Bee" for all to hear. Ethan just glared like she was about to kill his pet cat.

"Ethan, time to come inside. You're already late for group."

He glanced back, and I swear there was hope in his eyes—and pleading. I couldn't intervene, but he wanted me to. For the thousandth time that day, the boy pulled at my heart.

"It's okay, buddy. I think I'm getting tired anyway. We can work on other stuff next time," I said, hoping to get a smile out of him before he vanished once more.

"Can you come back tomorrow?" he asked.

"Let me talk to Dr. André. If he's okay with it, I'll do my best, but I need to get settled in my new apartment and think about getting a car. It may be a couple days before I can come back."

His face fell and took my heart with it.

"But I'll try," I said quickly. "You know, I really need to work on my base stuff."

I had no idea what base stuff might entail. What outfielder needed to work on tagging someone out at a base? It made no sense, but he was young and wouldn't—

"You play center. There aren't any bases out there. You just made that up."

Damn. Called out by a kid.

I chuckled. "You got me. Maybe I just wanted an excuse to come see my new best friend again."

His face transformed into sunlight. "I'm ... your best friend?" he said with a reverence only a child could possess.

I forced my face into grave seriousness and nodded. "The very best, Ethan. I really will do my best to come back tomorrow, okay?"

His gloved hand smacked into my back as his arms flew around my neck. The scent of grass, dirt, and child filled my soul. When he nuzzled my neck, I thought I might burst out into an ugly cry right there.

What the hell was happening to me? I'd never been a crier or overly mushy, but this kid was my kryptonite. It made no sense.

"Ethan! Come on now." The woman's voice was insistent.

"Go on, bud. I'll see you soon." I pulled him back and mussed his hair.

He waved his gloved hand, then streaked across the grass, where the woman shooed him inside then followed.

The playground had cleared out, so I wandered over to it and sat on a bench that stood watch over the yard. It had been a good day; accidentally so, but good. I chided my ridiculously bad sense of direction, then privately thanked myself for it. Maybe my subconscious brain chose to get on the southbound bus. Maybe I actually wanted to come back to the Ranch rather than go grocery shopping and spend the evening nesting in my new digs.

Who ever *wanted* to nest?

Well, *I* did, I grudgingly admitted, committing to a full conversation with the only person left on the playground.

"There's nothing wrong with nesting. I like feeling like I'm making a place my own, my home," I said aloud, to myself.

"Fucking weird if you ask me," a youthful voice with the edge of a warrior's blade said.

I whipped around to find the sullen loner from my first visit standing a few feet behind me. His stringy black hair hung limply to his shoulders.

"Oh. Hey. Thought I was alone," I said with a wry chuckle.

The boy didn't smile, but there was amusement in his voice. "Talk to yourself often? You'll fit into this place just fine."

I grunted, then mumbled, "More than you know."

When he didn't join me on the bench, I turned. His eyes were fixed, as though he was deciding whether I was a welcome sight or a blemish on the canvas of his world.

"I'm Nick."

"Yeah, I know."

I waited for him to introduce himself or say something more— tell me to screw myself, perhaps—but he just glared through a thicket of inky strands.

"What's your name?" I asked after the silence made my skin crawl.

"Why do you care?"

I shrugged. "I don't. Was just curious. It's better than asking myself."

"Aren't you here to blow sunshine up my ass? Tell me how much you care?"

"Nah. I don't even know you. I mean, other than you look like you just crawled out of House Slytherin."

He snorted at that, and a bit of his Teflon faltered. "I'm Noah."

"Not a very intimidating name."

He almost grinned. "Nope. Guess not."

"So, Noah, what's your deal?" I wasn't sure what I was doing or why I was digging into this hard case, but I loved riddles and hated unsolved mysteries—and Noah was as mysterious as they came. When I motioned toward the empty end of the bench, he strode over and sat. I took that as a victory.

"My deal? Is that some baseball psych thing?"

"No.   It's   an   annoyed-guy-staring-at-a-kid-try-ing-to-act-like-the-world-hates-him thing."

His eyes widened at the slap. It was soft, more of a tickle, but he took it as a slap.

"I don't know if the world hates me, but it isn't really my friend either," he said, his eyes drifting to his hands.

I let that hang in the air between us.

Several minutes later, he looked up. "You're good with him."

"Who?"

"Ethan. I've never seen him hug anybody."

That surprised me. He'd been so free with his affection, I'd assumed he was a hugger.

I shrugged. "I don't know. We just click, I guess. He's a cute kid."

"He's a great kid," Noah said defensively. "The best. Don't you fucking hurt him."

I squared our shoulders. "Excuse me?"

"I said—"

"I heard what you said. I'm asking why you said it."

He thought only a second. "Because I've watched that kid get his hopes up too many times over the years, then cry himself to sleep when he thinks no one's watching. I'm an asshole, but he's a good kid."

Huh. Tough, independent Noah wanted to protect Ethan. That was interesting.

"Why are you an asshole?" I asked.

He pulled back. "Fuck you. I just am."

I grinned. "Maybe I am too. Ever think of that?"

"Dude, really? You're a pro baller. Of course you're an asshole. That comes with the uniform."

I actually laughed at that—and he grinned.

"I guess it does for some players," I admitted. "But I hope not for me."

He stared, and his grin thinned into a line.

I turned back toward the playground and watched a streamer attached to monkey bars flap in the breeze.

"You coming back?" he asked after what felt like an eternity of pennant watching.

"Yeah, I am."

"Good."

Without another word, he stood and headed toward the building, leaving me watching his back and wondering what the hell had just happened. That felt like a rubbernecking experience, driving by a crash on the highway, slowing just enough to see that cars had collided but too quickly to have any clue what really happened. Before you knew it, you were past whatever the bottleneck had been, none the wiser.

Yeah, that's what it felt like.

I rubbed my neck, wondering if I'd scared him away or if something else had made him run.

"You get all the hard cases to talk."

I jumped off the bench so fast I nearly tripped over my own feet.

"Holy shit. Does everybody in this place specialize in sneaking up on people and scaring the crap out of them?"

André made a show of examining the ground around my feet, then walked around to look at my backside.

"I see no crap. Did you crap in your small clothes? Where is this crap?" His accent was both adorable and annoying.

"God, I hate you right now."

His smile reminded me why I stayed so long. "Welcome back, Nick. You are ... a welcome surprise. May I sit?"

I nodded and we sat. The bench was long, and Noah had pressed himself as far from me as possible, but André ... our knees touched. I couldn't stop staring at them.

"Do you have a fetish?"

My head snapped up. "What?"

"A thing for knees? You have been staring at mine."

Heat flooded my cheeks ... and neck ... and ears.

His fucking smile widened.

"Uh, sorry, I just, well—"

His hand covered mine, and the heat went from warm to inferno.

"I am very happy to see you again."

I croaked out, "Me too. I mean, you. I'm happy to see you too, again. Not me. I've seen me, you know, since last night. I was with me. Fuck."

He laughed, and I swear his mirth had a sexy accent. He squeezed my hand.

"How was your time with Ethan? He was very happy when he came in—once he got over his anger for being called inside."

My eyes darted from our hands to his eyes, and I had never been more thankful for a change of subject. I breathed in deeply. "It was awesome. He's such a fun kid, and smart. Did you know how smart he is?"

André nodded.

"We played for over an hour. I'm not sure his battery ever runs out."

"The batteries here are forever full. To be young again ..." His thought drifted on the breeze. "I am happy to see you, but this was a surprise."

"Yeah, sorry about that. It was a surprise for me too."

He raised a brow.

"I'm supposed to be at Kroger right now, stocking up. Tonight was a Netflix night, just me, the remote, and whatever came out of the microwave."

"That sounds nice—perhaps, except for the microwave food thing. Why did you end up here?"

"I kind of got on the wrong bus, then fell asleep on said bus, then woke up here."

It took a second to register, then he burst out laughing.

"What's so funny? I'm in a strange city. I got confused."

His laugh deepened. "Perhaps you should not get a car, after all. You might end up in Indiana on your way to the ballpark."

"Yeah, I could see that," I admitted under my breath, but not low enough to go unheard. He doubled over.

"You cannot be that bad, Nick. No one is that bad at directions."

I raised a hand and gave him the most innocent, sheepish look I could muster. "I am."

Mirth filled his eyes. "You are very cute when you pout."

"Hey! I wasn't pouting," I protested ... in a pouty voice.

"Your lower lip says otherwise," he teased, then gathered himself and whispered, "I have thought about your lower lip since last night."

The heat that filled my face moments before found its way into my chest.

"Really?"

He nodded, and his hand switched from squeezing to a gentle stroke, sending a shiver up my arm.

"André—"

"Have dinner with me again tonight."

I blinked.

"Let me cook for you—real food, not garbage from your microwave. I will show you what the French can do when they want something."

I blinked faster. "You want something? From me?"

"I do, Nick, and I think you want something too."

The heat blazed a trail southward.

"I ... André ..."

"Just say yes. I won't even make you take the bus to my home."

He said that last bit with a smirk. Sexy French fucker.

"Okay."

Sixteen

NICK

André hovered over the stove, cooing into his pot of French goodness like a mother bird urging her chicks to settle in their nest. I'd offered to help, but the only task he'd given me thus far was dicing an onion—and he'd taken the knife away and done it himself when my squares weren't all the same size. It sounded like chef snobbery to me, but I didn't protest.

He called the dish he was making chicken chasseur, and explained it was a French classic his mother made at least once each week when he was a boy. The simmering sauce, rich with white wine and who knows what else, filled the kitchen with an aroma unlike anything I'd ever smelled. If I could've opened my mouth and drank it in, I would have.

"Would you mind grabbing a bottle of wine from over there?" He pointed a wooden spoon at a door around the corner. I opened it to find a walk-in closet fit for a queen's shoes, but filled with racks and bottles. There were more than a hundred, slid neatly into cubbies from floor to ceiling. On the right side stood a head-high refrigerator filled with bottles of white and pinkish-looking varieties. The temperature reading was a perpetual display of wine chilled to perfection.

"Uh, André," I called out.

"Yes?"

"I think I'm in over my head here."

His snort echoed off the wooden panels of the hallway.

"Can you reach that one, on the top there?" His arm brushed my shoulder as he pointed above us both from behind. I could sense him almost pressed against my back, close enough to feel the electricity crackle, but far enough to long for his warmth. It was a heady, dizzying moment.

"Uh, yeah, I, uh, think I can, um, I can reach it." I had been reduced to word vomit.

His hot breath kissed my ear. "Excellent. I think you'll love that one."

My whole body tingled, but when I turned, sure his lips would meet mine for the first time, he was gone. I clutched the bottle to my chest, trying to still my sprinting heart, unable to stop beads of sweat from marring my brow.

"Come, pour the wine. Dinner is ready," André called out in his soothing, matter-of-fact tone, as if he hadn't just tickled my lobe with the feather touch of his breath.

As I filled our glasses, he set the massive pan-pot thing onto a hot plate in the table's center. I hadn't been allowed to see the holy dish since he added the last of the raw ingredients. He'd rapped my knuckles with his wooden spoon the one time I tried to sneak a peek. As he lifted the lid and sultry steam billowed into the air, I had to sit lest the sheer perfection of the fragrance bowl me over.

"André, what the hell did you put in that? It smells amazing."

"Just a pinch of *l'amore, mon* Nick."

Another thrill ran through me. I wasn't sure if it was his use of the word for love, calling me *his Nick*, the seductive tones of his irresistible accent, or the way my mouth watered as the chicken of the gods wept all over his kitchen. My brain couldn't register so many incredible inputs all at once, and nothing in me wanted a logical answer anyway.

"I hope you like this. It is special to me."

I looked up to find his eyes struggling to maintain my gaze. That was a first. He never wavered. Something in that simple, vulnerable moment made me smile.

"If it's special to you, I'm sure I will love it."

His tentative tone bloomed into teeth and parted lips, and eyes of ocean blue that almost made me forget about the feast laid before us.

I might've actually held my breath. His hand reached out and pressed into mine, and I shuddered.

"It has been a long time since I d—*cooked* for anyone."

Dated. He was going to say dated. Holy shit.

"I haven't dated in a while either," I said, letting him know I understood both his sentiment and his struggle. "Being a pro athlete, trying to climb that ladder, is hard enough without distractions. I know guys who try to juggle love and the diamond, but it rarely works."

As soon as the words left my mouth, I wanted to reel them back in. Had I just told him that I didn't want to date anyone? Would he think I wasn't interested? Would that make him think I wouldn't stay committed to helping Ethan too? Or would he think I was afraid of commitment to anything ... or anyone? My mind was spinning so fast, I thought it might take flight.

Then he spoke in his calm, reassuring voice, the one laced with just enough accent to make my knees buckle.

"We all must do what is right for ourselves. Our hearts know what is best. We only need to trust it." He squeezed my hand, then stepped around the table and sat opposite me. "Please, don't be shy," he said, gesturing toward the table covered with plates, platters, and bowls overflowing with green beans, potatoes, roasted onions and garlic buds, two different breads, and a bowl of some kind of dried fruit.

"It's just us, right? You don't have, like, fifteen others joining us?"

He chuckled. "I heard professional sportsmen had large appetites. I could not cook for you and let you go home hungry."

"No worries there." My eyes bounced from dish to dish. "If you cooked for me like this all the time, it wouldn't be my appetite we'd have to worry about being huge."

Dammit. Foot in mouth again. A nice, toasty rouge colored my cheeks.

His grin gained a predatory edge, and his eyes danced, but all he said was, "Oh, there is cherry cobbler for dessert. Don't save room. Just keep eating."

I moaned. "Coach is going to *kill* me if I come back from the off-season unable to wriggle into my uniform."

"You are *so* dramatic, Nick," he said as he ladled a ridiculous amount of chicken and sauce onto my plate. "This is not a fancy dish, but it is close to my heart. I hope you like it."

As the first bite fell apart on my fork, then melted in my mouth, I let out the most sexually satisfied groan ever made at a table.

"Should I leave you and the chicken alone? Are you having a moment?"

My eyes rolled back and closed as I savored the rich sauce.

"I think you need to rename this meal. How do you say 'happy ending' in French?"

André nearly spat wine across the table. "And here I thought I would be the one with the happy ending tonight, but it is the chicken who wins that honor."

He took another sip, and his eyes grinned at my expression of ecstasy.

"Wait, I know it now!" His voice was suddenly firm.

I stopped the fork as it rose to my mouth and looked up. "What?"

"This is what you mean by the phrase 'choke the chicken,' no?"

I gaped. The meat that had been stuck on my stilled fork broke apart and flopped onto my plate. André let out a deep, rumbling laugh and pointed his wine glass toward me.

"If you could see your face ..." His laughter swelled.

I didn't want to laugh, to give his terrible joke the satisfaction of my amusement, but his childlike glee was infectious. Before I knew it, my fork was resting on my plate and I was howling along with him. At what, I'm still not sure, but neither of us could stop laughing once it started.

"You're different when you're not at work," I said, when we finally came up for air—well, he came up for wine. I needed to breathe.

"How so?"

"I don't know. You're so reserved at the Ranch, so calm and reassuring, like nothing bothers you. Ever since we walked into your house, you've been ... I don't know ... relaxed? That's not right, but you know what I mean."

He grinned. "Truly, I do not. Please, try explaining it again."

"Now you're just being cruel."

He placed a hand over his chest. "I am sworn to do no harm. You know, the Hypocritical Oath."

I rolled my eyes. "I'm pretty sure that's a different promise than the one you made when you got your fancy degree."

"There you go calling me fancy again. Why does everyone think we French are fancy?"

"It couldn't possibly be your palaces, blinky towers, massive museums, and pride in your language that rivals most nations' patriotism."

"Our language is the most beautiful—"

"Your accent certainly is," I muttered a bit too loudly.

"Oh, you like my accent?" he said, thickening his vowels. God, he was sexy.

I blinked, then said quietly, "Yeah. I like a lot of things about you."

He set his glass down and leaned back. "You barely know me."

"And I would like to fix that." I took a fortifying sip, a bit larger than I'd intended. My head swam. "Tell me about the great Dr. André."

He tapped his fingers on the table, and I wondered if it was in annoyance or delight. Then he smiled. "First of all, it is Dr. André Luis Adolfo Martin."

"Ooh la la." I dabbed my lips with the cloth napkin he'd given me, then waved it in the air like I was being fancy.

He snickered.

"What would you know, Nick? I grew up in Dijon, a most beautiful town with the very best food in all of France. My parents still live there, along with my brother, Charles, and sister, Chloé. Charles is married and has one son. Chloé's most recent girlfriend is called Zoe."

"Chloé and Zoe? That's almost so sweet it's sickening."

His face darkened. "Oh, no, Nick. It is not sweet. It is the bitter pill."

I sat back, leaving him space to explain.

"Zoe is ... how should I say it ... not a great influence on my sister. She involves her in drugs and other things. It breaks my parents' hearts."

"I'm sorry," I said. "How long have they been together?"

"They have broken up many times but cannot seem to break free of each other. I believe they have been on and off for five years now."

I finished the last of my chicken and washed it down with the last of my wine. Swifter than a server in a Michelin three-star, André had my glass brimming again.

"And you?" I asked.

"Yes?"

Stubborn fucker, making me ask for everything.

"What about you? That tells me where you are from, about your family, but says nothing about who you are, what you enjoy, whether you've had great love or loss. Do tell. Inquiring minds want to know."

He barked a laugh. "You are too young to know that quote, Nick ." "Syndication says otherwise," I retorted.

"Touché." He raised his glass in salute, the twinkle returning to his eyes. "I am a simple creature. I love my work, my children. I run most mornings, and have competed in triathlons."

"Really? That's impressive."

He gave me that *it is what it is* French shrug. "I like to keep fit. My work sits me on my ass too much, so I do what I can in my free time."

"Still, that Iron Man stuff is the real deal."

He chortled. "I never said Iron Man, just regular triathlons. They are hard enough for me. There is no need to get mud in my hair." He ran a hand through his thick, wavy gray and black tresses like he was readying himself for the prom.

"I like your hair."

Where the fuck had that come from?

He smiled behind his wine glass. "*Merci*. I like yours too."

Now my hand flew to my unruly locks, self-consciously tangling along the way. He reached up and moved a curl off my forehead, eliciting yet another shiver. His fingers trailed the side of my face, then stopped and cupped my cheek. His touch was so light, I almost wondered if his palm was actually making contact. His eyes never left mine, never blinked or wavered. Without thinking, I pressed my face into his palm and closed my eyes.

God, his touch ...

His thumb stroked my cheek, and I let out a sigh.

"I like you very much, Nick, and would like to know you much more."

Seventeen

ANDRÉ

W hen Nick leaned his cheek into my palm, I thought my heart might burst. It had been years since I'd thought about another man, since I'd dared hope.

Yet here we were. This beautiful, kind, funny guy wasn't simply accepting my affection, he desired it. His eyes closed and I felt, more than heard, a rumble swell from somewhere deep within him, like the purring of a leopard, satisfied and at peace. He let out a deep sigh and his breath tickled the hairs of my arm.

I was a doctor, a scientist, a psychiatrist. I analyzed situations and people, their feelings and actions, their rational mind's voice and their inner child's cries. I gave guidance and advice based on data and information gleaned through process and control. My training taught me to never lead with my heart or allow feelings to cloud my judgment.

There was danger that came with that commitment to professional and medical precision. One's own creativity and expressiveness, one's emotional wellbeing, could become dulled to the point of being fully suppressed, like any skill that became lost to time and disuse.

But a heart was not a skill or a set of data, however much my logical brain might want to shove it into a neat box.

It was fire and rain.

It was a calm breeze and a raging tempest.

It was a tender touch.

And it made no logical sense—none whatsoever.

I couldn't pull my hand away. The warmth of Nick's cheek and his breath thrilled me, ignited a flame I thought had long flickered out. I'd never even tasted his lips, but they consumed my every thought. I let my thumb drift and barely graze his chapped skin; and with still-closed eyes, he pressed a tender kiss.

My world spun, my eyes watered.

This man I barely knew made me want ...

In that silent moment, with his lips pressed into my skin, I knew I would never get enough of his touch, of his longing, of his desire.

His eyes fluttered open.

His hand reached up and gripped mine. I sat frozen, transfixed, held captive by his gaze as he leaned closer, so slowly, then pressed his lips into my own.

Everything vanished. The Ranch, the children, the remains of our dinner strewn about the table.

There was only Nick.

He stood, our lips still together, and took my face in both of his hands.

There was a tenderness, a vulnerability, in his touch. It surprised me almost as much as the kiss itself.

I'd been alone for so long. So very alone.

"You didn't like me very much," he said, cruelly pulling our lips apart.

"What? When?"

His lips curled. "That first day, last week. You looked at me like I was going to eat your children rather than help them."

I lowered my eyes, but couldn't stop a grin. "Maybe. Eat is a bit strong, but I thought—"

"What changed?" he asked.

"You came back."

His eyes widened, along with his smile, and there were no more words.

We stumbled into the den, unwilling to part for even a moment, then tumbled onto the couch, Nick's weight pressing down on me. My hands wrapped around and trailed along the hardened muscles of his lean back as his tongue teased mine for the first time. He tasted of white wine and thyme.

I don't know how long we lay like that, entwined on my couch, lips searching, tongues wrestling. Our touch never grew beyond Nick's tender passion, never turned to hunger or lust. I couldn't stop tangling my fingers in his hair or squeezing his arms. Part of me wanted to rip his clothes off and devour him right there on my floor.

Yet even his caresses remained sweet and gentle.

I think that made me want him more.

He never made a move to grind or rut against me, though I felt him stiffen. I wanted to reach down, to stroke him through his jeans, to feel his desire, to fuel it, to drive him beyond—

"André," he said, pulling back. There was something tentative in his eyes—doubt or indecision? "I, uh, I haven't dated or, you know, been with anyone in … well, it's been years. Since college, I guess."

His gaze fell, then rose and met mine again.

"It's just …" His eyes fell away.

"Nick, we don't have to do anything tonight. It's okay. Being here with you, it's all I want."

His face became a kaleidoscope of emotions. I watched as he sorted through them, as his eyes flickered from me to somewhere in the distance, then back. I could almost hear his inner struggle, some great debate that had raged within him for years.

I wanted to understand him, to know him, to know what held him back, but he remained silent, and I feared to ask. Of all the things he could've done, stepping back from the precipice of desire was not one I'd expected.

Nick baffled me in the best possible ways.

I chided myself for the preconceived notions I'd created for him, the way I had assumed he would be like so many gay men, wanting casual sex as quickly and as often as they could get it.

Despite my attraction to the man, I'd assumed he had the emotional depth of a puddle.

Some objective observer I was.

Hell, *I* wanted that with him right there on my couch. If he'd asked or made the slightest move to undress, I would've thrown myself on him and given him whatever he wanted. I craved his touch, to feel his skin against mine, to run my lips and tongue and fingers over his nakedness. I wanted to take him in my mouth and swallow him whole.

It might've been a few years for him, but it had been a lifetime for me, and the way he looked at me …

"Nick, it's okay." I stroked the curl out of his face and watched it spring right back. "I am very happy kissing you."

He pushed himself up, hovered over me, and cocked his head. A quirky grin crept onto his face.

"I am very happy kissing you too, *monsieur*."

I couldn't stop a derisive snort. "That is the *worst* French accent I have ever heard. Please do not insult the language of love again."

His grin widened, and his accent worsened. "*Monsieur*, you wound me. I am very skilled at speaking the French."

I threw my head back against the cushion. "Why did I invite you into my home? Why?"

Without hesitation, he said, "Because you like my butt."

"What? I do not … I mean … what did you say?"

His mouth was twisted into a shit-eating grin.

"Don't play innocent with me, Doc. I saw you checking it out when I left with the guys last week, whispering with your friend, probably telling her how much you hated pro ballers. You were trying to be all Mr. Tough Staffer, hating on the poor volunteer, but I saw you glaring, lusting, drooling even." He pressed a palm to my chest and flicked his hair back like in a shampoo ad. "It's okay. I get it. My ass *is* fantastic. You can stare all you like. Talk to it in French, if that makes you happy."

"I will *not* talk to your butt, in French *or* English. That would be very strange, and I would fear its reply."

He snorted. "Oh, it's got comebacks. Loud, nasty ones, sometimes juicy. Maybe its French accent is better—"

"No. Don't you dare say your butt has a French accent."

"Well, it does roll its Rs pretty loudly."

I covered my face with my hand and smothered a laugh, torn between defending my mother tongue, throttling him, and shoving my tongue down his throat. "You are terrible. A vile, awful brute."

"A brute?" he spat out. "Are we in the fourteenth century now?"

"*Oui*! You are a medieval brute." I nodded. "A big, hairy one."

"Hey! I might be a brute, but I'm not hairy!" He yanked his shirt up. Abs glared back.

Sweet baby Jesus, his stomach ... My breath caught as I stared.

He pulled his shirt down and lifted a brow in triumph.

"I may be a brute, but I'm a *smooth* one, and you still like me, you French liker-of-the-brutes." His accent was a strange, almost offensively poor mix of German, British, and Chinese. French was nowhere to be found.

I groaned, then moved my hand so I could look at him again. His smile was wide, no longer snarky. The brown of his eyes had deepened in the lamplight. I wanted to tease or snap back, but all I could do was swoon.

"I do like you, Nick. Very much."

"Me too, *monsieur*." And he leaned down and kissed me again.

The yawling of a cat outside the window woke me. Somewhere in our couch fest, I'd ended up laying on top of Nick with my head nuzzled perfectly beneath his chin. We'd made out for what felt like hours, never removing a single piece of clothing, though I did sneak my hands into his shirt to feel his chest and abs. That nearly stole my will to hold back—until his self-satisfied smirk shattered the fantasy of the moment.

He wasn't a bulky bodybuilder with a neck thicker than his head was wide, but his chest was rounded and firm, making a heavenly pillow. He didn't wear cologne or aftershave, but I caught a pleasant scent of lavender from whatever soap he used. I'd enjoyed lavender in the past; that night, I wanted to eat a whole field of the stuff.

The rise and fall of his breathing lulled me to sleep like a babe in a swaying crib. I didn't remember when I'd fallen asleep, or if he had already drifted off before me. It was all a pleasant blur.

I hadn't noticed him wake as I did, either. Fingers gently stroked my hair.

"Hey, you," Nick said, a grin crinkling the skin around his eyes in the most perfect way.

"Hi." I kissed his chin, then glanced at the decorative clock above the mantle. "We passed out. It's one o'clock in the morning."

A small groan escaped his lips. "I'll have to call an Uber. The bus won't run this late."

"Nick, no. You do not have to do that. I will take you home."

He craned his neck to kiss my forehead. "You have work in a few hours. I can't ask you to do that."

"Having an off-season must be nice," I grumbled playfully.

He grinned. "It almost makes up for the one hundred sixty games and eight million travel days of the season."

"When you say it like that, I almost think you dislike it."

"Oh, I like—no, I *love* it. André, I wish you could know what it feels like to step onto a field with other elite athletes and thousands cheering." His eyes drifted, and his voice traveled to another time and place. "It's electric, but it's not all about fans fawning over me. They're fun, and my ego loves a good stroke as much as the next guy, but it's about the game. I've loved it since I was a kid, and now I get to play that game every day as my job. I get to be a kid for a living. One day, if I keep working hard and pushing myself, it'll give me a life I'd never have without the sport, a life few get to live."

The passion in his voice was infectious. I stared long enough for him to return to the present and glance down.

"What?" he asked.

I sat up on my elbows, careful not to spear his chest. "You're beautiful, Nick, in so many ways. You know that, yes?"

His cheeks colored.

"Hey, look at me." He reluctantly met my gaze. "You *are* beautiful, Nick. I didn't see it before, but I do now. Your love of baseball, your passion, most of all, your heart and spirit when you are with the children ... all of it makes you—"

"I'm just me, André." He squirmed beneath me, but I held firm.

"And you are beautiful. Thank you for giving me this wonderful evening."

"You're not the prick I thought you were, either, if that helps," he snarked, as I imagined him doing in the locker room. I chuckled.

"*Merci*, I think." I sat up straighter and stretched my back. "Unfortunately, you are right about me working in a few hours. That will require a lot of coffee. Would you like to stay the night with me?"

His eyes widened.

"Just to sleep, perhaps cuddle?" I clarified.

"Can I hold you while you sleep?"

My heart battered my chest. Nick continued to surprise me. We had only known each other a short time, but his passion was now clear. I had expected that with his sport, but when I'd seen it, several times, focused on Ethan ... I hadn't been prepared for that.

Then he turned his gaze toward me, and I was sure his fire would flicker out. As a forty-three-year-old man who had seen his share of life's challenges, I knew better than to hope this young, handsome man would even notice me. My analytical brain recognized my initial animosity for what it was: attraction wrapped in my own insecurities, tied off with a dose of jealousy. I'd erected a shell around myself, around my heart, and Nick had ignored it completely, pierced it with his smile, shattered it with his touch. I was the doctor, the professional, the one in command of his senses, but he'd crushed my defenses like they were made of clay.

And then, as we kissed on my couch, it was Nick who'd held back, who'd stopped me when I started tugging at the edge of his shirt. He said he wanted to wait, to get to know me better, to feel something special when we shared each other for the first time.

Since when does a twenty-three-year-old with all the horniness of youth raging through him become the mature, self-assured one? Wasn't he supposed to get all hot and bothered, attack me, tear off my shirt, and ravage me with his tongue? Young guys always wanted sex, right? They couldn't control themselves. They fucked anything that moved.

I wasn't a prude. I had no problem with a casual roll in the sack. Americans and their quaint notions of sexuality remained foreign to my ears, but I scolded myself for practically throwing myself at him like some whore in a dark alley. If he hadn't held back, we would've been naked and sweaty in seconds.

That wouldn't have been terrible. I'd dreamed of Nick naked more than once since we'd first met. God, those were good dreams. But Nick had paused. His eyes brimmed with so much more than lust; they were filled with quiet reassurance, and longing ... and hope.

What did he hope for? Was that gaze truly for *me*? I could scarcely believe it.

"I would like that very much."

He pressed his lips to mine and held us together for the longest moment.

When we parted, I struggled to my feet and held out a hand.

"Come on, let's go to bed."

The sun rose far too early that morning, streaming her vile happiness through the window before we'd enjoyed enough time in sleepy land. I woke to an unfamiliar pressure, a weight across my chest holding me down. Nick's arm snaked beneath mine and clung about my torso. The heat of a small campfire flickered against my back. I smiled at the idea of him pressed against me all night, and was nearly dizzy with lust as I felt his stiffness throbbing through his underwear against my butt.

I couldn't help myself.

Ever so slowly, I reached back and ... my god! He was thick and veiny and—wait, was he uncut? I couldn't tell for sure because any foreskin was pulled so damn taut, but I thought it was there. That made my heart race, and any drowsiness vanished. My own morning wood was no longer about having to pee, but I fled for the safety of the bathroom anyway, lest he wake and discover my moment of exploration.

My morning bathroom routine complete, I tossed on a t-shirt and shorts. I usually ran a few miles in the morning, but decided to only jog around the neighborhood then return to make us breakfast. If I couldn't have Nick's sausage, I'd make him one.

That thought made me chuckle.

"Hey, you. Where'd you go?" Nick was propped up in bed, his hair an utter mess and ridiculously adorable. He looked like a child who'd been woken in the middle of the night, still filled with dreams and grogginess—and I wanted to gobble him up.

"I went for a run to get the blood flowing, then cleaned up from dinner last night," I said. "Are sausage and eggs alright for breakfast?

We haven't talked about food you like or don't like. Is there a special baseballer diet I should know about?"

His sleepy, boyish grin sent a jolt through my chest.

"The only baseballer rule is that we can never get enough to eat." He caught himself, adding, "But after the table you set last night, I might have to amend that rule."

"I will keep that in mind." I sat on the bed beside him, took his hand and raised it to my lips. "If you would like to shower, the towels are in the cabinet over there. Breakfast will only take a few minutes."

His hands shot out, gripping my shoulders as he wrestled me into his lap so I was looking up at him. He brushed back my hair, then leaned down and kissed me deeply. I thought my whole body would melt in that moment.

"Thank you for a great night," he rasped, his mouth a breath away from mine.

I tried to reply, but words died in my throat. All I could do was stare into his eyes and remember to breathe.

After a moment, I sat up. "Those eggs won't scramble themselves. I'd better get to it."

"Okay, I'll take a quick shower."

I was setting the final plate on the table when Nick emerged in nothing but a towel wrapped around his waist. A light dusting of brown hair spread across his squared pecs, trailing down his lean torso and vanishing beneath the towel. I'd never hated terry cloth before, but damn that wrap.

He'd slept in a t-shirt, so this was the first chance I'd had to see him nearly naked. From the drops scattered across his chest and shoulders, he'd made a half-assed attempt at drying. I wanted to reach out and rip that towel off him, to dry those spots with my mouth, to ...

No, no, no, I told myself. *We are being good. Nick wants to be good. Stop staring at his nipples, so fucking perfect and pink. Why do they have to stick out and stare at the same time?*

But it was his hair that made me crave to touch him the most. He'd toweled off, but hadn't found the gel in my drawer, and his dandelion puff of a do sprouted in every direction—all except for that one curl that still fell across his right eye.

He was messy, unkempt, half-naked, somewhat soaked, and the most beautiful man I'd seen in longer than I could remember.

I nearly dropped my sausages.

"Um, hey."

"I know I said to be casual, but a towel?" I couldn't help myself. "Don't get me wrong, I could stare at you all day, but you might get cold, and I have to work this morning. I cannot stay to warm you up."

He blushed. "God, I'm sorry. I didn't mean to ... I mean, I wasn't ... I couldn't find your hair goop."

I barked a laugh. "Hair goop? What is this *goop*, Nick? I have been in the US a long time, but I do not know this word."

With one hand holding a precariously loose towel, he reached up and mussed his hair with the other and said, "Yeah, you know, the gooey stuff to make it lie down? My hair kind of has a mind of its own without it." The towel began to slip. His hair-mussing hand flew to catch it before it fell, and the pink of his cheeks turned bright red.

My grin widened. "It does like to stand on end, I see, except for your rogue curl. It's adorable."

He devolved into a small boy, head bowed, eyes bouncing from one foot to the other, feet shifting so he had to work to keep up with the bouncing—and his cheeks were on fire. One hand abandoned its towel duty long enough to brush the curl back.

It immediately fell into his eye again.

The poor, adorable man.

"The hair goop is on the middle shelf of the medicine cabinet. There are several varieties. Use whatever you like." Mischief was a devil I knew well. "Or ... you could simply sit and eat. I rather like the view."

The blush flared, and his whole upper body turned crimson. "I'm, uh, gonna go do my hair thing with the goop and stuff."

He fled before he'd finished the last words.

As he passed the fridge, his towel finally won its freedom and dropped to the floor. He bolted and let out the most hilariously girlish squeal—and I caught my first glimpse of the world's most perfect ass.

Eighteen

Nick

I locked the bathroom door and stared at myself in the mirror. Had I really just lost my towel in André's kitchen?

Lord, help me.

I actually like this guy, and we agreed not to get naked for now. What's the first thing I do the next morning? Fucking flash my ass at his sausages. Or sausage. Okay, that was funny. Embarrassment turned to amusement, and I found myself laughing at my reflection. A chuckle turned into a giggle, then an uncontrollable round of belly laughs. I reached back to brace myself, but the shower was just out of reach. My balance slipped and I toppled, ass-first, onto the cold tile floor.

If my laughter hadn't been out of control enough before, it was then. Tears were streaming down my face. I wasn't even sure why I was laughing, but the range of emotions I'd experienced over the last twelve hours, topped off by the towel incident, had finally caught up to me. Laughter wasn't an option. It was in command.

"Nick, are you alright in there?" André's voice drifted through the door. The handle rattled, but didn't open. I'd locked it.

I'd locked the door so my naked ass could use hair goop.

I laughed harder.

"Nick?"

"I'm okay. Sorry. Everything just ... the goop ... and the towel ... and your sausage ..."

"Most men love my sausage, Nick."

Tears flowed into an ugly cry. "Please don't make me laugh harder. I'm dying in here. And I'm still naked and frizzy."

"We cannot have frizzy. Naked is fine. In fact, if you prefer never to wear clothes in my home, that would be lovely. I saw your bum, but not your sausage."

I groaned through a snort. "You are evil. Cruel and evil, Frenchie."

"My country has gone to war over nicknames. Be careful with your words."

Shit, that made my side hurt.

"Go away. I'll be out in a minute. Now I need to pee and your floor is starting to look inviting."

"No, no. I will go. No peeing on the tiles. They are yellow enough." Accented laughter, if there was such a thing, followed his footsteps as he left me in peace.

God, I hated him.

Snot was streaming, tears were dripping, and my formerly clean, naked butt needed another shower from its time on the tiles. Just great. Fantastic first impression, Nick. Nicely done.

I stood, found the aforementioned goop, did my best to tame my hair, then looked around the bathroom for my clothes ... which were in the bedroom, on the other side of the locked door, where André might walk in when he heard me emerge.

So, I did what any mature man would do in that situation: I listened through the door.

Nothing.

The sound of André singing in French was a distant echo. The coast was clear.

I shot out of the bathroom, found my clothes, and leapt into my underwear faster than a young Marky Mark during a wardrobe malfunction on a runway.

But in my haste, my left foot missed the hole and I fell onto the bed, undies dangling from the other foot.

André chose that moment to check on me.

"Oh, my dear Nick, are we going back to bed so soon? I could certainly trade what's on the table for what I see here."

I rolled onto my stomach and wriggled my way into my underwear, nearly shoving my nuts into my lungs. Sweet Jesus, that hurt. Privates covered, I stood and shook my jeans out, then finished dressing.

André leaned against the doorframe and watched like I was putting on a show.

"Come, let's eat before it gets cold." At least he had the kindness of heart not to rub my blush-filled morning in my face. I swiped at the wrinkles on my t-shirt and followed him back into the kitchen.

"Coffee?"

"Yes, please," I said. "Black."

He glanced around with one brow raised. "Interesting. Black coffee, coming right up. Help yourself."

I turned and froze, staring at the table. André didn't know how to portion control. Seven different dishes stared back at me.

"This looks amazing. Did you cook all this while I was in the shower?"

He set a mug down in front of me. "Yes, it was nothing. The cheeses and fruits were already cut. I just arranged them on the plates."

We went about the business of piling eggs, potatoes, sausages, croissants, fruits, and cheeses onto our plates.

"Is food a love language?"

He cocked his head. "Food? I have never seen it described this way."

I shoved the hot, flaky bread into my mouth and let my eyes roll back. "It is now. You may have to marry me before breakfast is over. This is amazing."

"I do my best." He chuckled, but I caught a glimmer in his eyes. A moment of silent eating passed before his tone shifted. "What you have done with Ethan is nothing short of remarkable, Nick. Thank you again. Sara also passes along her thanks."

"Thanks. That means a lot, although I'm not sure I did anything special."

"It was very special. Ethan has struggled for some time, even before going silent. It has only been a few days, but his behavior has improved. Each time you visit, he takes another small step, and he has been more open in our sessions than at any time I can remember. If you did nothing more than help him open up to me, it would have been wonderful."

I tried not to look away, but André's praise made ants crawl across my skin. "He's a good kid. I think he just needed a friend."

André set his fork down and leaned back, staring at me. "You are a good friend, Nick. I see that now. It is a beautiful thing."

"So, I've been wanting to ask, do you think it would be okay if I came back to see him on a regular basis? The off-season lasts until March, so I have lots of free time."

He thought a moment. "Let me talk with Sara and Dr. Marber. The Ranch has a policy of only allowing family members to visit children, and only during specific hours, but we have bent the rules in the past. I think this would be an ideal time to do so again."

André grabbed his fork and resumed eating.

I sat in frozen silence, picturing the days I'd spent with Ethan, his little laugh, how he brightened when he saw me each time I showed up. A warmth filled my heart with those visions.

"I didn't even want to come," I muttered.

"What? When?"

"That first day, with the guys. I'd just moved here, hadn't even moved in, really. The visit was on the books and they asked me to join. I couldn't really say no to my new teammates, but the last thing I wanted to do was a charity event on my first real day in town.

"Then we came, and I saw all the kids, and Ethan came up to me; snuck up on me is more like it." I grinned at the memory. "Even when he didn't say anything, his smile ... André, his smile lit up the room. He has such a strong heart. I can see it. Under whatever else is there, he is such a great little boy."

André's gaze lingered, then a tiny smile curled his lips.

"He thinks a great deal of you too."

Nineteen

Nick

André had to work, so I figured I would catch the bus back to my apartment so we could both start our day, but he insisted I stop by the Ranch to say hi to Ethan and Sara. I understood the nod to the boy but was surprised when he brought up his co-doctor. It sounded as if he wanted me to spend time with her, for us to get to know each other, and I didn't think that had anything to do with Ethan or their approval of more time spent with him. I'd dated a bit before getting drafted, but no one had ever wanted me to snuggle up to their friends, especially ones they worked with. This was new. And sweet. And *very* André.

Ethan nearly bowled me over, Sara wrapped me in an unexpected embrace, and André grinned through it all like a happy drunk on a sidewalk corner. It was the perfect start to a beautiful day.

By the time COTA[1]'s finest delivered me a block from my doorstep, it was almost noon. What began as an early start with near-naked towel shenanigans had quickly stretched into a half-day affair. I grabbed the

---

1. COTA: Central Ohio Transit Authority, the public transportation system in Columbus, Ohio.

last of the bread and peanut butter in the cabinet and made a quick sandwich. The grocery store had missed me far too long.

Sandwich eaten and stomach thoroughly unsatisfied, I changed into my workout clothes, packed a bag with a shower kit and clean outfit, and headed back to the bus stop. My mind wouldn't stop showing me André's smile and grinning eyes. I needed to pump some iron and clear my head.

There were only a few cars in the massive lot outside the stadium. The front office didn't get an off-season like we did, with trades, the next draft, marketing, and a million other running-the-business-of-baseball things to maintain. I didn't give those lonely vehicles a second thought as I strode into the tunnel.

What I hadn't expected was the crashing sound clanking out of the weight room. I figured the other guys had either traveled home for the rest period, or belonged to local gyms. Who wanted to come back to the stadium for a workout? The traffic alone would deter me if I had a better option. Yet here I stood, peeking in the tiny window, watching Kervin spot Zack as he bench-pressed a small car's weight. Zack's seventies disco queen hair hung limply, drenched in sweat, and his shirtless body revealed rippling muscles I'd only seen in quick flashes in the locker room.

Pumped and primed, he was a beast. Damn.

And Kervin ... holy cow, he looked more like he'd just stepped off the cover of a magazine than worked out. Blond hair blew in the air-conditioner breeze, and his toned body glistened with a light sweat. He even flicked his hair back when it fell across his face, reminding me of some perky commercial on TV. The pair of them together in the weight room was porn without the sex.

"Get your ass in here," Kervin shouted through the door when he caught me pulling a peeping Tom.

I startled and pushed the door open.

"Dude!" Zack sat up as the weights settled in the bracket. His chest heaved. "We thought everybody bolted after that last game. You still in town?"

I nodded. "Yeah. Nowhere else to be, and I figured off-season would give me time to get to know Columbus. What are you two still doing here?"

"We live here," Kervin said. "We should totally hang out. Zack's dad runs this big company and set us up in the sweetest pad with a pool and game room. It's awesome."

"A pool? In Ohio?"

Zack nodded. "Yeah, it's kind of over the top, and it sits empty, like, six months out of the year."

"But it's awesome after a workout. Jump right in and feel the sweat and pain drift away," Kervin added.

"Uh, sounds nice."

"No more rest," Kervin snapped at Zack. "Another set now or I'm adding weight."

Zack groaned, then looked up at me and mouthed, "Save me, please."

I chuckled, shrugged, and watched him lay back and push through another grueling set.

An hour later, I was soaked and wobbling around the weight room more than a Weeble on a countertop. Leg day sucked.

Kervin and Zack were just finishing a round on the treadmill, their usual cool-down after a hard weight routine. They staggered over to the bench where I'd sat and was praying to the leg-day gods to make the lactic acid stop searing the core of my being.

"Okay, out with it," Kervin demanded without preamble.

I looked up, confused.

"You've been smiling during leg day. Nobody, not even your overly hot roommate, smiles on leg day."

Zack added, "Yeah, you get laid or what?"

I rolled my eyes and laughed. "No, I did not get laid, thank you very much. I haven't even been in town a week. You think I'm humping everything that moves on Grindr or something?"

They shared a look, then shrugged in unison. "Sounds like a fun play for fresh meat."

"Fresh me—"

"Don't play coy," Zack said through the towel now pressed into his face. "You're not bad looking, a pro baller, somewhat—well, not stupid—"

"Hey!"

"Okay, reasonably not stupid."

"Definitely not stupid," Kervin clarified, adding no clarity to anything.

"Wow. I've known you a few days and this is what I get?" I feigned offense. This was a locker room. We were teammates. Most importantly, we were dudes. This reckless banter had been part of our DNA since we wielded clubs and dragged meat back to the cave.

"What you're going to get is an invitation to our place for dinner, but only if you tell us what you've been up to that's got you looking so pregnant." Zack's towel dropped and he scrunched his face to underscore his point. It just made him look like a cartoon character with massively frizzy hair.

"Fine." I tossed my towel across the room into the bin, then turned my naked ass toward them to reach into my locker. "I went back to the Ranch."

A deafening silence blared behind me. I tugged on my jeans and turned back to find them both staring, monumental blankness smeared across their normally cocky faces.

"You're smiling because you ... went back to a kids' home?" Kervin asked.

I nodded and tossed a fresh shirt over my head without a word. Taunting them was fun, and oh, did they deserve it.

"You went for what? To see a kid?" Zack asked slowly.

"Yep," I said, my head popping through the neck hole. "Remember Ethan? You might not've met him. He's an eight-year-old who hasn't spoken for a few months."

"You went to see a kid who doesn't even talk?" Kervin sounded like a kindergartener sounding out words.

"He does now."

Two heads tilted at exactly the same angle at exactly the same time. I had to bite back laughter.

"Guys, Ethan came up to me when the group was there last week. I didn't go looking for him. When he wouldn't talk, I guess I took it as a challenge, said some silly stuff, made an idiot out of myself. Before he ran off, he told me his name."

"His name?" Zack asked.

"That's it?" Kervin added.

"That's not *it*. That's everything. Ethan hadn't spoken, not to any-one, in months. Telling me his name was a breakthrough. When I went back a couple days ago, he chatted my ear off."

"How many times have you been back?" Kervin asked.

"Three. I was there yesterday too. Oh, this morning may count as four. I was only there for a quick visit, but we did hang out and throw a few."

"You were there last night and this morning?" Kervin asked. "And you threw a few? Baseballs? With the eight-year-old?" Zack added.

God, they were easy to lead around by their noses. This was fun.

"Yep. You got it. That's why I'm smiling. Text me your address. See you around six?" I asked over my shoulder before marching out of the locker room without waiting for an answer.

I had just enough time to grab a bus home, then walk to the grocery store, get my kitchen sorted, and head back to the bus stop. A car was quickly moving to the top of the week's agenda.

I knew the guys' house was just north of downtown. No player wanted to live too far from the stadium. What I hadn't expected was for the bus trip to last a whopping twelve minutes. I hopped off a block from their address and gawked at the houses surrounding me. One side of the street held long rows of townhouses that looked like perfectly neat books made of brick and stone sitting on a shelf. The other side of Fifth Avenue was a young girl's dollhouse fantasy come to life. Neatly manicured lawns and ancient trees surrounded houses of wood and brick whose age was impossible to guess. Each one I passed was different, unique in shape and design, unlike the suburban cutouts I'd seen in many of Nashville's neighborhoods. It felt like walking back in time.

I reached the address Zack had given me and nearly fell over. The mansion-sized, regal structure held court at the corner of Fifth and some unnamed side street that was actually cut off by a sidewalk and curb, effectively making their house a corner lot on only one street. On the southwestern corner of the house, where two walls would normal-ly meet, rose an onion-domed tower topped with a steeple-like spike.

Three rows of tall windows offered anyone inside a nearly one-hundred-eighty-degree view. Arched brick painted a faint lime green were held aloft by white columns that surrounded a deep porch.

The other houses along the street had been impressive. This one was breathtaking.

"Hey."

My head snapped to the porch, where Kervin stood, one hand rested on a column.

"Hey," I said, stepping up and handing him a bottle of wine. "I wasn't sure what you liked to drink, other than beer. Hope this is okay."

He glanced at the cheap grocery store wine and smiled. "This is perfect. As long as it's red, I'm good. Zack likes more foofy drinks. Feel free to give him shit."

"One order of shit, coming right up, sir."

He grinned and clapped me on the shoulder, ushering me through the front door. "Welcome to our casa."

The outside of Casa Zack and Kervin had not prepared me for what lay beyond the threshold.

"Holy shit," I said before realizing my mouth was moving.

Elegant wood trim that matched the glimmering floors cut angles on every wall and corner of the spacious foyer. The entranceway was large enough for a round table that could have doubled as a dining table to sit in its center atop a plush rug and crowned by a massive bouquet of cut flowers. My mouth fell open as I looked up some twenty feet at the stately chandelier that looked like something they'd stolen out of the White House back in the 1800s, only its candles had been replaced by delicate-looking bulbs.

"Yeah, I did that too, the first time we came here. I thought Zack's dad was pranking us when he said he'd already bought it and handed us the keys. He kind of went overboard, but we love it here."

"Kind of?" I was nearly speechless as my eyes fell on the ornate wooden banister that wrapped around the *Bridgerton*-esque staircase. "K, this place is ... Damn. I don't think I've ever seen anything like it."

I felt his hand on my arm as he pulled me into the next room.

"Let's say hi to Zack and I'll take you on the tour. He'll get pissy if you don't kiss the ring."

I nodded absently as we strode past a fireplace made of stacked stone and butterfly wings. Okay, it was just stacked stone, but from what I'd seen so far, I wouldn't have ruled out the butterfly fairy's involvement in crafting this place.

An old-world-meets-modern vibe slammed into me as we rounded the corner into a galley kitchen long enough for a cruise liner. The rich, polished flooring and trim I'd seen in other parts of the home continued into the kitchen, but was now accented by the thick black-and-white marble of the counters and a long butcher's block table in the room's center. The table's surface was a swirl of colors and shapes, mesmerizing in its own uniqueness and beauty. I'd seen something like it on a TV show a while back. The guy from *True Blood*, the werewolf, had one made for his Dungeons and Dragons room. Apparently, rich people had rooms for their games, and this guy needed a cool table for his. Now Zack had one. Shit.

Shiny silver appliances with touchscreens brought everything into the twenty-first century, but were virtually invisible when nested within antique cabinets whose faces were carved as ornately as any statue in any museum.

"Dude!" Zack called, glancing up from whatever he'd been stirring on the stove. "Glad you made it. Make yourself at home."

I raised a hand in a weak wave. "Thanks. Your home is really something."

He beamed. "Yeah, we're really happy here." He looked at Kervin. "Babe, give him the tour. I need another thirty minutes or so."

"Yes, dear." Kervin set the wine on the swirly table. "Want something to drink?"

"Yeah. If the tour is like the entrance, I might need one before this is over."

He grinned and opened a glass door, displaying all manner of liquor bottles. "Pick your poison," he said with a game-show assistant's wave toward the bottles.

"Got any beer in that fancy fridge? Do you tell it what you want and a robot butler retrieves it?"

"Zack told his dad we wanted a human butler who only wore thongs, so we didn't get that option with our fridge." He snorted as he opened the refrigerator door. "Blue Moon, Stella, Heineken ... uh,

I think that's Edinger in the back ... and there may be one Corona, but we're out of limes, so that's out."

I shook my head. They had more beer in their fridge than the brewpub we'd eaten at.

"Blue Moon's awesome. Got any oranges?" I asked, testing the bounds of their hoity-toityness.

"Bro, what do you think we are, barbarians? Of course we have oranges, and they're already sliced." He reached back into the fridge, then turned and shook a sandwich bag with several wedges of neatly cut orange in my face.

I whistled. "The service in this place is awesome."

"Drink your juice, Shelby," he said, shoving the orange-wedge-topped bottle at my chest, then popping the cap off a Heineken and taking a long pull. "Come on, let me show you around before Chef André over there ropes us into doing work."

My skin prickled. *Did he just say André's name because he knows something?* I thought, scrunching my brow.

On cue, my phone chimed.

My twentysomething motor reflex took over and the device was out of my pocket and unlocked in one motion.

> **Doc André:** Hey, you. Thanks for coming to the Ranch this a.m. Ethan's been babbling about it all day. We might need your magic touch to turn him off again.

> **Doc André:** Oh ... it was nice waking up next to you too. And sleeping with you. And you holding me.

> **Doc André:** And have I told you how masterful your towel-handling skills are? I've hidden all the others, so you'll just have to drip-dry next time.

I snort-laughed at the screen, and the widest, goofiest grin parted my lips.

"Oh shit. Babe, we've got a live one over here," Kervin said, elbowing Zack to make him turn around.

"What?"   I   protested   in   the   lamest you-just-caught-me-with-my-towel-down squeak.

"Oh wow," Zack said. "He did meet someone."

"Here we thought he was being a saint taking care of children, but he was getting dick on the side," Kervin added. "We need details, you sneaky cocksucker. You did suck a cock, right?"

I wanted to be annoyed, but André had never texted me before and I was too giddy to scowl.

"Babe! Look at that face!" Zack waved a spatula. "He didn't just get dick, he *likes* somebody."

I set my beer down, dropped my elbows between swirls on the table, and rested my face in my palms. Through a groan, I said, "Fine. I met somebody."

"I knew you were full of shit at the gym," Kervin said, pointing accusingly. "Out with it. No secrets in the circle."

"There's a circle?" I asked, hoping to throw them off, even for a second.

"Yeah, this circle. We're the gays on the team and we've got to stick together, no matter what. Marcus is part of the circle, but the straight edge, so we're more like a cir-square."

I snorted. "A cir-square?"

"I'm a baseball player, not a geometry teacher. Fuck it. Now, who is this man and where did you meet him?" Kervin asked.

"And why no dick? We want dick," Zack punctuated.

This was hopeless. I straightened and shot back the rest of my beer—which was more than half the bottle. Kervin and Zack's eyes widened.

"His name is André."

"Oh shit!" Kervin said. Zack's face remained blank.

"He's one of the staff doctors at the Ranch."

"Wait, is he the older guy with the wavy gray hair? The one who's always watching us from the corner when we visit?" Zack asked.

Kervin nodded. "That's the one. He's sexy, in an age-gap-romance epic sort of way."

"He's not that old," I protested.

Kervin's brow nearly hit his hairline.

"He's not!" I said, a little too defensively. "He's forty-three."

That's when I realized he was nearly twice my age, and my smile slipped.

"Aww. Did Puddin' just do the math?" Kervin teased.

"Babe, stop that," Zack whispered, then turned to me. "Tell us about him. How'd you meet? I need to stir while you talk, so ignore my back being turned."

Kervin crossed his arms and gave me a you'd-better-start-talking stare like some interrogator in a spy flick, while Zack turned and tended to dinner.

"There's really not much to tell. We met last week when all of us did that thing for the kids. I spent more time trying to get Ethan to talk than anything."

"Ethan's the kid, right?" Zack asked without turning around.

"Yeah. He's eight. Smart little guy." I grinned thinking about him. "Anyway, like I told you at the stadium, I went back to see him again, took him one of the team-signed balls and a glove. You should've seen his little face. It was like I'd set his world on fire. We spent that afternoon playing catch. That's when he started talking for real."

I told them about André thanking me for helping with Ethan, how we'd gone to dinner, then about my accidental trip south the next day.

"You got on the wrong bus and didn't notice until you were outside the city?" Amused disdain laced Kervin's voice.

I shrugged. "I fell asleep. Besides, I could get lost pretty much anywhere. Don't ever let me drive unless you're giving me turn-by-turn."

"Got it," Kervin said as he dug another couple beers out of the fridge and dressed mine with an orange. "So, you slept over but didn't even see his baguette?"

"I'm pretty sure a dick would be sausage or some other meat, not a loaf of bread," I snorted. "And no, we didn't go past first base. Lots of making out, a little touchy-touchy, but all above the belt."

"Well, that sucks," Kervin said.

Zack shoulder-bumped his hubs. "Babe, not everybody thinks with their cock."

I took my opening to shift things off me. "How long have you two been together?"

They shared a glance and both of them grinned.

"That depends on who you ask and how you define the word *together*," Zack said.

Kervin rolled his eyes, but only so I could see. "We met when we were drafted onto the team two seasons ago. Being the romantic in our coupledom, I say we've been together since that first day because there's been no one else but Zack since."

Zack scoffed. "And I say it was months later, when I stopped hating him long enough to go to dinner. He was such an arrogant little shit throughout spring training and the opening. I couldn't stand to be in the same room as him most of the time."

"But you checked out my ass in the locker room," Kervin said.

"And your chest and arms and cock," Zack said dreamily.

Kervin slapped a palm to his chest. "Not my cock! How dare you."

"Every chance I got." Zack laughed, then looked over his shoulder at me. "Don't you love how our showers don't have walls?"

"Uh, I hadn't really thought about it, but sure," I said, though in truth, I had reveled in that discovery on my first night with the team. Watching Marcus lather himself was as close to a sexual experience as I'd had all year. It was like watching a perfectly tanned, but more muscular, statue of David cover itself in bubbles, rub them all over, slowly with one hand, then the other, wet its hair and sling it back and forth ... then, ever so slowly, rinse the bubbles from its taut, rock-hard ...

I totally popped a boner thinking about it. Why did my straight roommate tear me up so badly? If the swirly table hadn't been in the way, Kervin would've busted on my bulge.

"And who says you're the romantic in our marriage?" Zack snorted. "You don't cry at movies, you don't leave me cards or notes or flowers, and you don't even cuddle after sex unless I grab your arm and hold it hostage."

"I'm a hot sleeper. You hate me sweating all over you," Kervin countered.

"That's true. You are a furnace."

"And I don't leave you little notes in your luggage because when you travel, I go with you. We're on the same team, silly," Kervin said.

I took a sip of beer while they bantered back and forth. I hadn't really been around a ton of gay guys, and even fewer couples. It was fun to see how they played off each other. As different as they might appear, they were a matched set in my book.

Which made me think of André again, how easily we talked and teased, how effortless just being together was. I knew it was silly to be smitten after two dates, but I couldn't stop smiling. The way he looked at me in mock horror when I spoke with a French accent was one of the funniest things I'd ever seen—and it made my chest swell.

"Uh, hello, over here," Kervin said, waving a hand like we were a hundred yards apart rather than staring across a swirly table. "You got that dumbass goofy look again. Were you thinking about Dr. Bread Dick?"

Zack spat the beer Kervin had just fed him. "Shit, now our pasta has beer in it."

"Beer makes everything better, babe," Zack soothed, then turned to me. "So, baguette got your goat?"

I tried not to laugh. I really tried.

"Fine. Yes. I was thinking about André."

"Aww," they said in unison.

"Assholes, I hate you both," I huffed.

"I think I said something like that right before Kervin asked me out and fed me his mighty loaf," Zack said with a wink.

"You might get a little baked goodness shoved up your oven later for that, sweet thing," Zack growled.

"Ew, gross. And bread doesn't work. We've been over this. Dicks are meat." I sounded like a twelve-year-old girl who'd been told she couldn't have Skittles.

"Forgive me if I don't take you for the dick-is-meat expert since you haven't even seen your doctor naked," Kervin said, determined to out-ponytail me. "Let's go do the darn tour so my little lover dove can finish dinner without drowning it in Heineken."

"Aw, lover dove. That was sweet. I take back everything I said—except the oven part. You sweat in bed." Zack pecked Kervin on the cheek.

"I'm going to vomit. Where's the bathroom?" I asked.

"First stop on the tour," Kervin said, like he was speaking through a microphone.

Safely ensconced on the throne, I swiped my phone alive as fast as my thumb would move and typed. I read my message, then erased it, and typed again. Five attempts later, I hit send.

> **Me:** Is it too much to say I've been thinking about you today? Like, a lot.

> **Me:** Oh, God, I said like, like I'm a valley girl. I'm totally turning into that girl over you.

> **Me:** Shit, I said like twice and totally. This is all your fault. I blame the French!

Apparently, Kervin and Zack had put me in a funny, bantery mood, which translated into my first text messages to André. Lord, help us both.

> **Doc André:** You can storm my Bastille anytime, Towel Boy.

I didn't totally get the Bastille reference. It was a prison back in the day, whatever day that was, right? I wasn't sure why he had one or why I would storm it, or what that even meant, but I was pretty sure it was sexual because, well, we were guys.

Towel Boy I understood. Little shit.

> **Me:** I'll have you know, my towel-handling skills are unmatched. You threw me off with all your post-run sweat and breakfast goodness.

Doc André: So, you like me sweaty?

Me: No, I like you smelling like eggs and sausage.

Doc André: Oh, well played. Someone's in a mood tonight.

Me: Yeah, being around Kervin and Zack will do that to anyone.

Doc André: Your teammates? They were here last week, no?

Me: No. I mean, yes. No, yes, they were there, and they are my teammates. Anyway, I ran into them at the stadium gym earlier and they invited me to dinner.

Me: How was Ethan today?

There was a pause before the dots danced again.

Doc André: He is wonderful, Nick. I am just so happy you are in his life.

Me: He's a special boy. I really like him.

Doc André: I can't decide which I want more right now, to tease you with my French or my tongue.

Me: From Ethan to French kissing. I might need a subject change bell next time.

Doc André: DING! I want to see you naked again.

Me: Please don't make me hard again.

Doc André: Again? Did you get hard thinking about me at Zack and Kervin's home? Nick, that's the sweetest thing you've ever said to me. It's our first distance boner.

Me: You're worse than the guys. I need to go before they think I fell into the toilet and break the bathroom

door down. Can you please get towels with Velcro?
Better yet, I'll bring a robe next time.

Doc André: Next time. My two favorite words today.

I clicked my screen to darkness and finished my business, determined to stop grinning before I left the bathroom. Kervin would only
get worse if he knew—

"Tell Dr. Bread Dick you'll text him later. I know that's what you're
doing," Kervin chirped through the door.

The boys were irreverent, relentless, and offensively beautiful.

All reasons I knew we'd become the best of friends.

Twenty

André

It had been a long day at the Ranch. Someone must've put something in the water because the kids were wound up—not simply a few, but all of them. I'd been working with youth long enough to have a very long fuse, but the rascals nearly reached the hot end of it today.

When I got home, all I wanted to do was pour a glass of wine, flop onto the couch, and watch mind-numbing reality TV until my eyes wouldn't stay open. My stomach had other plans, grumbling louder than the children's day-long screams that still made my cranium pulse.

Thankfully, when I opened the refrigerator, leftovers from the breakfast I'd made for Nick that morning stared back at me from the top shelf.

"Breakfast for dinner it is," I said, pulling out the remains of the no-longer-crispy potatoes and all the other goodies I'd cooked. Most of it was salvageable. Wine would make the rest better.

"First things first," I said to myself, setting a filled wine glass and bottle on the side table by the couch.

After a moment of careless spooning and tossing of foods, my plate and I fell into the comfort of leather-clad cushions, and I flipped on the TV. A local news show had reached the nightly sports report and was prattling on about some hot guy in a white-and-blue uniform. I was too busy pushing eggs and sausage about my plate to listen—until

I heard one of the men say, "... Clippers will make a number of off-season trades."

I'd made it nearly an hour without thinking of Nick, but that line had me sitting ramrod straight in no time, my mind consumed with images of him in those butt-squeezing pants.

Are they trading Nick? He just got here. Would they really do that to him? My mind spun, but I'd never even watched baseball, much less understood the intricacies of the game's business end. I listened attentively, but the men on the screen spoke in some foreign tongue. All I could think about was calling Nick so he could tell me it wasn't true, it wasn't about him.

Then my rational brain, the one longing for me to focus on dinner rather than a man I barely knew, kicked me in the gonads.

Does it even matter? He's a fun time, that's all. It's all it will ever be, no matter where he lives.

I was a doctor. I wasn't supposed to suffer the voices in my mind arguing. *Merde*, they weren't even supposed to speak.

You're nearly twice his age, André, old enough to be the guy's father. He's twenty-fucking-three years old, you cradle-robbing idiot.

Damn, my mind was in a cruel mood.

He's hot, young, intelligent, compassionate, sexy, and a million other things that don't include any interest in a gray-headed old fart like you. I hate to tell you, but you are past your prime, and he's way out of your league.

Images of Nick flashed before me: standing outside the Ranch's gate, playing ball with Ethan, smiling as I cooked, turning eight shades of red as his towel slipped. My heart ping-ponged so fast ... I took a sip of wine, then another.

Even if he's not getting traded, you know he's going to make it into the majors and get moved to who-knows-where. He'll be popular, famous, and surrounded by fawning fans. Men will throw themselves at him. He'll have his pick of the hottest guys, all closer to his age, and you won't even be an afterthought. What are you thinking?

Was my subconscious—which wasn't very *sub* tonight—right?

Was this stupid?

Why would Nick even want to be with someone my age when he could have anyone he wanted? Even if he got over that gap, his life would never be settled, not as long as he wore a uniform. There would always be fans and men wanting his attention. He would never control his own fate, not truly. Teams traded players all the time. It would be like some poor military spouse, moving constantly, or struggling with a long-distance relationship that never settled in one place long enough to *be* anything.

I set my plate on the table, suddenly no longer hungry. My glass, however, got refilled—to the brim.

The news blinked away, replaced by an advertisement for deodorant. A baseball player swiped his underarm with a stick and smiled at the camera. He was gorgeous, fit, and wonderfully shirtless. Nick would probably like him. He would definitely like Nick.

What was I doing?

I downed a quarter of my glass.

Then an ad for a local car dealership screamed through the speakers. All I heard was, "Call us now." Something in that phrase made me glance beyond my glass. The actor then said, "... or text us at ..."

My phone buzzed and dinged. Nick.

I snatched up my phone faster than a shortstop snagging a line drive.

Twenty-One

André

I didn't see Nick again until Saturday, which was three days without him visiting the Ranch, three days of me pining out the window, hoping to see his face pressed between the bars of the gate. I was pitiful.

But Ethan was worse.

Every time I passed him in a hallway or on a stair, he asked, "Have you heard from Nick? Is he coming back today? I didn't bring my glove, should I go get it in case he comes?" and a hundred variations of those same questions. While it was wonderful and cute to see his enthusiasm, and finally watch him act like a normal, somewhat-adjusted eight-year-old, I was getting close to pinching his nose to make it stop. I didn't care when a child asked, "Why?" a dozen times—I was used to it—but Ethan was asking about Nick, which made *me* think about Nick. Remarkably, there were moments when I'd managed to focus on work and put him out of my head—until Ethan asked again.

Saturday morning finally arrived, and I drove into the city. It was my first time seeing where Nick lived. I'd braced myself to enter a bomb shelter, based on his description of minor league players' incomes, but was pleasantly surprised to find he lived in a neat, cookie-cutter apartment complex with three buildings made of well-maintained brick. The annoying part of my brain that reminded me of his early twenties-ness—every hour, on the hour—warned that the interior might be more like a dorm room than an adult living space. Thankfully, there were no dirty clothes piles or moldy food scraps anywhere in sight.

"Hey." His face brightened when he opened the door and found me standing outside. "Come on in. I just need to throw on some shoes."

I nearly passed out when he leaned in and kissed me before darting back inside to retrieve his sneakers. How could such a simple gesture turn a seasoned professional into a puddle of melted Jell-O? It was like I was stuck in a Lifetime movie crammed with puppies, kittens, and Eskimo kisses.

"Any idea what you want?" I shouted down the hall while scanning the den for debris that wasn't there.

"I don't need anything fancy, just something reliable for around town."

"No road trips planned?" I asked, hoping to get some insight into the player trade story without having to ask directly.

"Nah," he said, appearing from his bedroom. "It's not like I have anywhere to go. Besides, I just got here, and I like being settled. It's time to nest a bit."

My heart skipped a beat.

He handed me a few pages filled with website images. "I did a little research on Marcus's computer. There are several dealerships nearby with specials running. Mind if we check them out?"

I grinned. "My day is yours, Nick. Just tell me what you desire, and it shall be."

His brow rose almost as quickly as his grin, then he laid a hand on my chest and inched his mouth as close to mine as he could get without touching, and whispered, "Careful, Doc. Don't promise more than you can give."

A shudder raced through me.

My mouth opened, then closed.

I felt dizzy.

Then his lips made contact and sunlight burst through me.

"Let's go—cars before boys," he said, leaving me teetering on jelly-filled legs.

We made it to two dealerships before Nick's hunger reared its ever-present head, so we stopped at a local diner neither of us had tried. Worn-looking staff ambled about the place, tattered checkerboard tablecloths blanketing tables and booths. If the place hadn't been filled with happy-looking diners, I might've suggested we try a place with less, I don't know, battle damage.

Despite my misgivings, the food arrived quickly and steaming, and was surprisingly good.

"Oh, you have to try these," Nick said, savoring a mouthful of something called fried grits. The very notion of a fried grit, whatever that might be, offended my *sensibilités françaises,* but his eyes were closed as he chewed, so I smiled. I hadn't expected his hand to shoot up, filled with cheesy, gritty vileness. A wave of something—that feeling you get when you spin too many times then attempt to walk—crawled across my skin. Which assumed that skin could get dizzy ... but that's beside the point. Feeding one's date a bite at a public table was such a simple gesture, yet in that moment, it held me in awe. As Nick's fork reached my mouth, our eyes met, and I was sure he felt the moment's import too.

"Oh, that is delicious," I said appreciatively, surprised the words escaped my lips.

He grinned and nodded, scooping up another bite and shoving it into his mouth.

It was only then that the simplicity of our morning struck. We'd driven around town, shopped for cars, and were now eating a meal together. I tried not to read more into things than were present, but it felt so easy and comfortable, like sipping hot tea and savoring its warmth as it traveled down one's throat on a nippy morning.

Being with Nick felt that way.

I'd almost made it through that pleasant thought without my subconscious kicking me in the rear, but a twentysomething guy who'd apparently just worked out sauntered by our table in his tank top, shorts, and musky sweat. I glanced up, then back, just in time to see Nick follow him with his gaze. My rational brain watched him glance up, then return to his plate quickly, but the other part of me spoke first—and loudest.

Told you so. This is a losing battle. Nothing good comes of this.

I was about to excuse myself with some pretext about washing my hands when Nick looked up and said, "Today's been really great. You've chauffeured me around all morning—and that's a French word—so technically, I've been using French all morning. Or have I been using a *Frenchman* all morning? I'm not sure."

Two fingers flew to my forehead faster than I could stop, but a grin tugged at my mouth.

His playfully frustrating, shit-eating grin glared down at me. "Seriously, today's the first normal day I've had in forever, and, I hope you won't hate me for saying this, but ... it's because I'm with you."

The darn diner spun again. I reached for my water glass only to tip it over, dousing Nick's plate a split-second before doing the same to his shirt and jeans.

"Oh, Nick. I'm sorry." I leapt to my feet, searching for a server who might help.

He looked down at his jeans, then up at me, and the little shit said, "You really will do *anything* to get me out of my pants, won't you?"

What does one say to that? In the middle of a diner surrounded by people wondering what klutz just threw water on his poor guest? How should I even respond?

"Oh, honey, let me help with that," our octogenarian waitress said, bending down and slamming a towel into his lap, missing his kibbles and bits by only a fingernail.

"Uh, thanks, ma'am. I'm okay. I can—"

"Nonsense. You just sit there and let me rub you off."

Nick's smugness was soaked up by her towel, only to be replaced by wide eyes, tight-lips, and reddening cheeks.

That did it.

I doubled over in my booth, right there in front of half of Columbus. Tears streamed down my face as Nick stared in horror at the grandmother patting much too firmly and far too closely to his goods, the one section of denim that had actually remained dry.

"Thank you so much. I'm good now," he said, lifting the lady up by her spindly shoulders. "I'm going to run to the bathroom."

He darted away without daring a glance in my direction. I wagered he'd never run to first base that fast, and I was practically hyperventilating.

A couple minutes passed before my breathing returned to normal and I no longer felt uncontrolled chuckles welling within, then my phone chirped.

> **Nick:** You are going to pay for that, Frenchie. You let an old lady rub me off in public!

If anyone else had called me that, I would've been angry and offended, not because it was a slur on my homeland, but because it just pissed me off. Coming from Nick, after what he'd just experienced, it made me bark a laugh loud enough to turn heads. When I read the second sentence, I snorted loud enough to earn glares.

> **Me:** I am still thinking about you saying I wanted your pants off. Is that an option now? Were you offering? I will be sure to throw water on you more often if that is all it takes.

> **Nick:** Jesus, what am I going to do with you?

> **Me:** Take your pants off and find out. It's not called a French kiss for nothing. You Americans just put it on the wrong body part.

The dots danced, then froze, then danced again.

Nick: If I wasn't afraid our waitress would try to join in, I'd tell you to get back here and rip my clothes off now.

Me: Wait. You're not into little old ladies with disgusting towels? It looked like she had a firm hand.

Nick: Her hand was definitely firm. And, no, I'm into little old men with disgusting mouths. Know anyone like that?

I tried to ignore that he'd just compared me to an eightysomething woman. The fact he'd acknowledged our age difference and still made things sexual sent my pulse racing. Okay, he didn't explicitly acknowledge anything, but he'd referenced it, and that, from an objectively psychological standpoint, counted.

Horseshoes and hand grenades. Look it up.

Me: Do you know how bad I want you naked?

Nick: Let's get this car thing out of the way so we can spend the afternoon answering that question.

Me: I can order you a car on my phone. We can skip the dealerships, go straight back to your apartment.

Nick: Wow. Are all Frenchmen this horny?

Me: You have *no* idea. Wait until you see my beautiful baguette.

Nick: NO! NO! NO! NO! NO! What is wrong with you people? A penis is a meat, not a bread. NEVER a bread.

Me: Um, Nick, why do you hate the loaf? Do not hate the loaf. The loaf is your friend.

Nick: If I didn't like you so much, I'd hate you right now. Don't you *dare* admit to Kervin you said any of that or I'll ... I'll ... I'll ignore your baguette for as long as I can stop staring at it.

Me: I'm confused at your bitterness toward a manly brioche, but will respect your wishes. I cannot have you ignoring my *Crème De Le Crumb*.

Nick: I don't speak French, but I'm pretty sure you just cracked a joke. You will pay later. I am not one to take offense lightly.

Me: Are you challenging me to a duel?

Nick: I have a sword. You have a pastry. We'll see who wins.

Nick: Now stop distracting me so I can finish drying my jeans. This hand dryer is taking forever when I have to stop and text every two seconds.

The image of Nick standing in the bathroom with his jeans held to a hand dryer sent me cackling so hard the waitress came to check on me, thinking I might be choking. When I told her what he was doing, her hoarse laughter mingled with mine, a harmony that greeted my poor baseballer when he returned to our table.

"I don't want to know, do I?"

The waitress, who I hadn't noticed to be the sharpest knife in the block thus far, didn't miss a beat: "Honey, if you wanted someone to blow on it, you should've just asked while I was down there."

Twenty-Two

Nick

We hit three dealerships after lunch. By the time we walked onto the third lot, I was getting frustrated, but André's persistent smile and playful banter kept me in a good head space. In the end, I purchased a 2021 Nissan Leaf. I'd seen electric charging stations at both my apartment and the stadium, so saving on gas made sense.

It was cheap and had plenty of room in the hatchback for clothes and gear, especially since the back seats folded forward to expand the carrying capacity.

But the thing that really sold me was how the previous owner had ordered a custom paint job in the coolest blue, somewhere between royal and midnight.

"This isn't a standard color. You won't find it on any other Leaf," the salesguy said, trying to make one leaf sound different to every other one on the tree.

"Isn't that the same blue as what's on your jersey?" André asked, pointing at the hood.

I leaned down, then looked back at him. "How do you know that? You're not even a baseball fan."

He shrugged and thickened his accent so every *th* sounded like a horribly tortured *Z*. "I know *zis* guy on *ze* team."

For the first time all afternoon, the salesguy was speechless.

A decade later, when the paperwork was done and the keys were resting in my sweaty palm, I turned to André and declared, "He shall be called Leif."

André and the salesguy shared a glance, then burst out laughing.

As I turned to fold myself into the driver's seat to drive away, André looked up and down the car's frame, then eyed me head to toe, as if he was making some critical comparison.

"Look at *ze* little bug. *Zis* is almost as cute as you are, Nick," he teased, his *Z*s crying out in pain.

I turned, refusing him the satisfaction of my grin. "He's a Leaf, not a bug ... and his name is Leif."

André snorted.

Stupid Frenchie.

"Get in. Leif wants to burn some rubber. We can grab dinner while we're out."

I could *hear* his self-satisfied smile behind me, but he said nothing as he climbed in and clicked his seatbelt. "I am all yours."

I reached over and patted his knee. "I know."

My hand didn't leave his knee as we drove, and it only took a few turns before I felt his tentative touch warming my skin. He didn't hold my hand so much as caressed it the entire time. That was somehow more intimate, more intentional, than if he'd simply gripped or laced or whatever guys did when handing for the first time. Maybe I was reading too much into a simple gesture, but it made me feel special. If I hadn't been driving, I would've leaned over and kissed him right there in Leif.

Instead of a lip-lock, would that have been a Leif-lock?

God, I was turning into a sap.

I found a Mexican restaurant that looked like its roof was about to cave in and led us to two empty parking spaces. André stood, clutching his door and eyeing the building like it might come to life and transform into a giant cockroach.

"Nick, are you sure—"

"Come on, you snooty bitch, the run-down places always have the best food. I bet this turns into one of our favorite spots."

His head snapped toward me, and something I didn't quite understand flashed in his eyes. It was soft and gentle, with a dash of hunger.

What had I said?

"I would like ... well, having places ... going to a regular ..."

I'd never seen André stumble over his words. It was horrifying—and *hysterical*. Part of me wanted to help him, to throw him a lifeline, but the prankster player in me was cracking up inside as he writhed.

So, I cocked a brow and leaned against Leif.

"I will give this"—he waved a dismissive hand toward the restaurant—"a try."

Something in his tone, his posture, his eyes, told me those words promised far more than a meal.

As the server cleared the last of our plates, I sat back and rubbed my stomach like I was a sumo wrestler who'd just devoured his slightly smaller, but equally round, opponent.

"I love a good chimichanga. What do they put in that cheese? Crack? I could eat it all day."

André smiled. "And you would waddle all the way around the bases."

"Don't make me laugh. It hurts." I chuckled and nodded. "Hey, when did you pick up on baseball? Last I checked, you avoided anything related to organized sports."

"I never said that, only that I did not follow them closely. I never had a reason to ... until now."

He took a sip of his margarita and eyed me over its salty rim, mischief and fire brimming in his eyes.

I held his gaze, savoring his playfulness. His hair was slightly disheveled from our time on the lots, the wind having its way with him most of the day, but his eyes were in perfect order—orbs of the purest blue drawn from the depths of some hidden lake, high in the mountains, where no other color dared intrude. His royal blue shirt only stoked the flame of their perfection.

"You have a reason to like team sports now? Do tell."

He took another sip, this time a longer one, then lifted his chin and set his glass down, like some ancient king about to pronounce a sentence.

"Nick, we French do not beat around bushes like you Americans love so much, especially when matters of the heart are ... when something is important."

"Am I important to you?" I asked, fully understanding him, yet still needing to hear it aloud.

He reached across the table and took my hand. I stared down, unable to move.

"We have not even known each other two weeks, and you consume my mind, Nick. At home, at work, when I run, you enter my thoughts without any invitation. You need none. My heart longs to see you, to hear your voice ... to feel your touch."

He seemed to struggle for his next words, despite those flowing so freely. The last of his margarita vanished, then he dabbed his lips dry before meeting my gaze once more.

"I believe my children would say I am very much 'in like' with you, Nick."

I'd been swooning a bit until he said that. A half-restrained, utterly childish laugh flew out of my mouth. I quickly covered it with my other hand as my eyes flew wide.

"I'm sorry. I wasn't laughing at you, or what you said. It was beautiful, really. That last part was just funny, and very much what your teenagers would say."

He gave me a wistful smile and nodded, but remained silent.

It was my turn. No more beating around bushes, as he'd said.

"I really like you too, André. You have surprised me at every turn."

He exploded into a laugh, and I nearly leapt out of my seat in surprise.

"I surprise you?" he asked. "*Mon dieu*, Nick, I am very good at reading people—it is my profession—and I have never been so wrong, and so pleasantly surprised, about a person as I have been about you."

I smirked. "Thought that highly of me last week, did you?"

"Not ... exactly, no." His eyes fell, like a dog caught chewing on shoes. "I made some assumptions that proved to be somewhat ... well, I was wrong."

"I like you all uncomfortable and squirming. Please, continue," I teased.

This time, his eyes flared and his teeth appeared.

"You are incorrigible, Nick Dunlap. Why do I like you so?"

"Because I have a fabulous French accent."

He groaned and held his palm to his chest. "You wound me, sir."

"I'd rather do other things to you."

His head shot up. "Yes?"

"Let's go home."

The dealership had fully charged Leif before I picked it up, but the little kid in me, ever enamored with new toys and anything with buttons, had to stop and plug it into the EV charging station near the front of my apartment complex.

"You run out of charge already?" André asked before his window finished lowering.

"Nope. I just wanted to see how this thing works." I held up the plug that looked more like a gas nozzle than an electrical connector. "This is so cool. The car actually locks this thing into place so nobody can yank it out."

"Someone would want to siphon your power? Is that a thing?"

I shrugged. "No idea. But they can't!" I shoved the thingy into the port doohickey and grinned at the *Star Trek*-like chime that sounded when the lock engaged. "*Voila!*"

André rolled his eyes. "Do you two need some privacy?"

"Maybe. He is kinda hot." I stroked Leif's hatchback like it was, well, a man's back. "Hang on. Let me grab my things out of my car."

The moment I settled into the seat beside him, André reached over and grabbed my hand. He held it, without saying a word, as we made the less-than-one-minute trek to my apartment door. I'd held guys' hands before, but something about how André silently claimed mine made me nervous.

He'd made it clear all day, especially at the restaurant, that his feelings for me were growing. The way he'd described it, we'd quickly crossed the line from crush to ... something else. That made me nervous too.

I'd never been in a relationship, unless a two-date college fling or a one-night off-season hookup counted, and I was pretty sure they didn't.

I'd only really crushed on one guy, the catcher for my college team. He was a grad student who'd sat out a year due to injury, and everyone looked to him for guidance, like his one year of extra life experience made him a sherpa with pearls of ancient wisdom to dispense. He was wicked smart, but I doubted he had a llama stashed in his condo.

But the wisdom thing, the idea of it, the thought of him having more experience, that drew me to him. He always knew what to do, how to act, what to say. Nothing rattled him.

Confidence might be sexy, but stability and steadfastness were smokin' hot.

And his ass. God, his ass was perfection wrapped in sensuality dripping with lust.

But my crush wasn't about the physical, despite how nice that had been to stare at. I was lost in his gaze the moment we met. Then he spoke, and my world spun.

If only he'd been gay.

That memory reminded me of Marcus. I hadn't spoken with him since he left, and that error needed to be corrected.

André lifted my hand to his lips. "Are you going to invite me inside?"

"Is this a vampire thing? Because, if it is, I may have to reconsider."

He snorted. He had a cute snort, kind of French and piglet mixed together.

"I do not want to suck your blood, Nick; however—"

"Yes, please come in and suck whatever you like. *Le suck e moi.*"

"You will pay for your desecration—"

My lips stopped whatever faux offense he was about to spew.

"Come on," I whispered a moment later. "This armrest is killing my ribs."

He play-slapped my shoulder, then kissed me again. I swear I could *feel* his smile in my chest.

The moment he set foot into my apartment, I turned and pressed him against the inside of the door, letting our weight press it shut. I grabbed his wrists and held them above his head, then leaned my body into his.

"You drive me crazy, André. You know that, right?"

He tried to kiss me, but I dodged, intent on an answer.

"I ... I hope so."

His uncertainty astonished me. This beautiful, brilliant man couldn't tell I was crazy about him, that my crush was probably more annoyingly Disneyesque than his? I rubbed my cheek against his, ever so gently, teasing our stubble against each other.

"Nick—" he rasped.

"André." I brushed his lips with mine, pulling away when he craned forward. "I'm so 'in like' with you it hurts. I think about you when I'm working out or running errands or hanging out with the guys. I dream about you."

His brow rose.

"Yes, *those* dreams, and you rocked my world—and made my sheets messy, thank you very much."

His snort returned, and he squirmed to free himself, but I held firm.

"Let me show you how much I like you, André. Please."

He stopped struggling and stared into my eyes. "Only if you let me do the same."

Twenty-Three

André

Words lost all meaning as our lips met.

I expected Nick to be aggressive and rough. I'd braced myself to be tossed onto the bed, or thrown against a wall as he devoured my mouth and tore off my clothes. I'd thought about our first time so often it hardly felt like a first time.

But it was.

And Nick was nothing like I'd expected.

His lips were soft and firm, his kisses a breath on the wind. His only touch, fingers dancing across my cheek, hovered more than pressed as they passed above my skin.

His movements were expressions—no, intentions. I could feel his need and desire, his passion and fire, all the feelings that flowed so freely through his eyes each time our gazes met.

There was no force or urgency. There was only affection and tenderness.

I melted against the door. The weight of his body pressing into mine held me upright. My weakened knees couldn't have survived his first kiss.

"Nick—" I breathed as our lips parted.

"No more talking."

He stepped back and gripped my hand, pulling me along behind him. I blinked and we stood before his bed. I'd lost time as we passed through the apartment. Was this another dream?

Warm hands slipped beneath my shirt, lifting it over my head.

"André ..."

I startled from my waking dream to find him staring at my chest. His eyes lifted to find mine.

"You are beautiful."

His fingers traced the lines of my pecs, pausing briefly to tease each nipple. He swirled his fingers along the pattern of my salty hair, sending thrills across my skin. Then his feather touch found my stomach.

"You never told me you had abs," Nick said, feeling his way around each one, like he was fingerpainting their outline. "I might not want to take my shirt off now."

He glanced up, his eyes dancing with the playfulness I'd come to adore.

"I believe we had a deal, *monsieur*," I said.

"Yeah, for my jeans. We never said anything about my shirt."

I couldn't take it anymore, so I reached down where he knelt, gripped his shoulders, and pushed him onto the bed.

"Hey!"

I moved too fast for him to protest, straddling him and grinding my ass into his groin.

"Oh, damn. If you keep that up—""No more games. Lift your arms," I ordered.

Nick's eyes widened, and slowly—ever so slowly—his arms raised above his head. I grabbed the bottom of his shirt and yanked it over his head, then tossed it across the room.

"You were worried about me seeing *this*?" His perfectly rounded, chiseled chest and obscenely cut abs glared up at me.

He smirked. "This old thing?"

"You are a tease, I think."

"Try me. You might find I follow through on my threats of a good time." His playfulness was more of a growl.

So I called his bluff, unbuttoning his jeans in one smooth motion. Before he could move, I scooted down, unzipped his fly and pulled from the bottom, discarding the denim as quickly as I had the cotton a moment earlier.

"No underwear?" I asked, as I stared at his twitching cock and drooping balls.

"Hate it. My puppies need to roam."

God, I loved his mischievous silliness.

I crawled back up his legs and took one ball completely in my mouth.

"Oh, fuck, André—"

My tongue swirled around it, taunting the hairs, tasting his musky skin. My hands slipped beneath him to grab his butt, kneading. When I felt his fingers dive into my hair, I moved up and ran my tongue along his shaft, slowly tracing the purple veins pulsing along its length. He twitched, then his body convulsed as I reached his head, tickling the sensitive skin just beneath.

"André, damn, that feels so good."

And then I took him in my mouth. There was no tenderness, no gentle touch, no passionate kiss. My mouth dove on his cock, devouring it to the base. He jerked upright, but I pressed him back down. With one hand, I held his balls, gently tugging on them, while my mouth moved up and down, lips pressed against him, tongue probing and teasing.

Up and down.

Again and again.

"Oh, shit, André—"I pulled back and released him. "Not on your life. Not yet."

He stared up at me, eyes wide. I swore I could see his heart pounding in his chest.

I grabbed his legs, shoved them back, then threw my tongue into his crack.

"Oh, damn!" he called, as my tongue pierced his hole.

I ran my teeth along the inside of his butt and was rewarded with a shiver, then dove back into him, pressing my tongue deeper and deeper. With my hand, I grabbed his cock and stroked him, careful to avoid the head and make him come.

"André!"

I drove faster, harder. Gripped him firmer.

"André, fuck!"

I pulled away, returning to my straddling position above him. His arms were above his head, gripping the headboard, flexing his taut muscles. Sweat beaded down the center of his chest, and his eyes were nearly rolled back.

"Take your pants off, please. I want to feel you naked against me," he begged more than asked.

So I stood and wriggled out of my pants, then dragged my boxers slowly down and off.

"Holy mother—André, that thing is huge!"

I shrugged, but couldn't suppress a proud grin.

He reached up and gripped my cock, as if inspecting some fruit at the grocery store.

"Oh, I want that," he said.

I leaned down and kissed him. "It's all yours."

When his lips wrapped around me that first time, I swore the stars had fallen and filled the room. He sucked like he kissed, tender and gentle. His hands gripped my hips and pulled me further up the bed so I straddled his chest, and I nudged the pillow under his head. He craned forward and took me in his mouth again. One hand gripped my base, while the other roamed my chest and stomach. There were so many sensations: tickling, teasing, sucking, pressing, slamming into me all at once.

"Fuck, Nick, I'm close!"

He gripped me firmer, moved faster, thrust me deeper down his throat.

"Nick!"

His fingers dug into my chest, as mine gripped his arms. My whole body shook, and I lost the last of my control, spilling myself into him in wave after wave of pleasure.

But he didn't stop, didn't let a drop escape, kept drawing me in and out until I became so sensitive I had to pull back.

"This was supposed to last a lot longer," I said, flopping onto my back beside him. "I was going to do that for you."

He propped himself up on an elbow and faced me. "Who says it's over? We have all night."

I smiled and cupped his cheek. "Yes, we do."

Twenty-Four

Nick

I woke before André at some ungodly hour when the sun was peek-ing half-lidded over the hills outside. He was usually the chipper chap to rise early and welcome the day with a smile and some other dose of annoying positivity. Why I rose with the new day's birth was a mystery, but for once in my life, I was glad for it.

We lay tangled together, a mess of limbs and sweat and dried mem-ories of a passionate night. André's eyes were closed, his dreams racing across darting eyes. The room was stuffy, and the covers lay discarded at the foot of the bed. I let my eyes roam across André's pale skin, buried beneath a light blanket of fur. The hair on his head grew thick and full, and still clung to its original black color—at least half of it did. He had more salt than pepper, and would clearly lose that battle in the coming years. The curls on his chest had surrendered to time before we'd met, and pure silver gleamed in the dim light of my room.

His arms weren't corded or thickly muscled like those of my athlete brothers, but they were lean and firm, like the rest of his body. Tiny pink nipples, like Easter eggs poking out of the snow, peered up, the only color on a pale canvas. The contrast between my tanned skin and his beautiful lightness fascinated me. I wanted to touch him so badly, nibble his nipples, swirl them with my tongue, pinch them and make him squirm, but he still slept, and shenanigans were no way to greet the day.

I couldn't help but continue my tour. When else would I have free rein to simply study my ... my what? What was André to me now? *Friend* felt so inadequate. *Lover* made me sound like some glamorous motion-picture star from the time before color in film. We clearly weren't boyfriends. I'd never had one of those, and I wasn't sure I'd even know where that line was much less when we crossed it ... *if* we crossed it.

He was my André.

I smiled.

That sounded so possessive or clingy or ... I don't know ... like I was falling for him.

Was I? Was I all of those things? Was I falling?

He shifted in his sleep. His eyes never opened, but he turned onto his side facing me. The slapping of his cock against his leg drew my eye. Lord, that thing was a Louisville Slugger if I'd ever seen one. I'd sure held enough of them—the bats, not the penises.

His Weimaraner was fully shrouded in its sweater, all snug atop his furry sack, like some turtle who'd fallen asleep with its head barely peeking out its shell.

Nipples be damned, I *really* wanted to touch his turtle.

I could still taste him. Like a perfectly balanced dish, he was salty and sweet, earthy and ... fuck, he wasn't a wine or a steak. What was I thinking? I chuckled at my own silliness; what I thought was my inside chuckle, but apparently wasn't.

"Hey, you," he said in our traditional greeting.

The moment our eyes met, a smile parted his lips. He was bleary-eyed and wild-haired, and I couldn't imagine a more beautiful sight.

"Morning," I said, leaning over to kiss him.

He pulled back and a hand shot over his mouth. "Bad idea. I have horrid morning breath."

I grabbed his wrist and pulled his hand away, then pressed my lips to his.

"Nothing will ever stop me from kissing you."

He blinked several times, and his brows creased, then relaxed, then creased again. I could see a million thoughts playing in his eyes; a movie fast-forwarding ... to the good part? Or the tragic part? Or the ending?

"Nick—"

"Let's get cleaned up. Unless you have other things to do, I'd really like to spend the day together again."

He drew in a breath and held it. His eyes focused so intently, I wondered if he was trying to see through me.

Then his fingers found my cheek. "I would like that, very much."

"I just have one request."

One brow rose.

"I know going into work is the last thing you want to do on a day off, but can we visit Ethan? I haven't seen him in a few days, and, well, I just want to ... I guess I miss him. Does that make me terrible? It's terrible, isn't it?"

Now he really did study me, so long and hard my skin began to melt under his diligent eye. He sat up and turned to face me with crossed legs. His hands found mine, and he raised them to his lips. When his gaze rose, moisture rimmed his eyes.

"Nick Dunlap, you may be the most wonderful man in the world. Of course we can visit him."

I'm not sure why I felt so self-conscious asking that. Neither he, nor anyone, at the Ranch had offered the slightest objection to my prior visits. Maybe it wasn't the visit that made me uncomfortable.

Maybe it was the *missing* him.

Was it normal to miss a child like that? It made sense for a parent or uncle or brother to miss their son or daughter or whatever, but I was none of those things to Ethan, just some ball player who'd shown up and didn't know the first thing about helping troubled kids.

"He misses you too. He says so as often as his little lips move." A wry smile crept onto André's face. "Sometimes, when our need is great and a lifeboat passes by, we reach for it. We cling to its ropes and haul ourselves onboard. The mind does the same thing, Nick—as does the heart."

"You think he's clinging to me? He sees me as, what, some kind of safety?"

"Perhaps. But perhaps you are seeking a raft of your own, no?"

My mouth opened to protest, to question, to ... I didn't know, I couldn't think. What was he saying? Did he think I was lost too, that I was troubled like Ethan?

He squeezed my hands gently. "Why have you never spoken of your family to me?"

My eyes fell to our clasped hands.

The stuffy room was suddenly unbearably hot.

"I don't have any to talk about." My voice was distant in my own ears, an echo from the past I barely remembered.

André simply sat and watched, his hands never leaving mine. That felt safe. It rooted me in place. Without his touch, I would've fled.

"I grew up in rural Mississippi, outside Madison. Frank, my father, was a sheriff's deputy. When he drank ... he wasn't himself."

I waited for André to stop me, to interrupt so we could start our fun day, but he sat quietly, patiently, his tenderness urging me forward.

"I was so little, maybe four or five. That's the first time I saw him hit her."

"Who? Who did he hit?"

"My mother." A tear brimmed on my lid, and I swiped it away, refusing to give it power.

"Why did he hit her?" André asked gently, his voice a balm.

"I don't know. I don't remember. She was in the kitchen. I was sitting on a step just outside the screen door. I don't think either of them knew I was there. Words became shouts, then screams. I remember sitting there, unable to move or run, covering my ears with my hands, squeezing my eyes to block out the world. He kept hitting her, André. He wouldn't stop."

Other tears broke free. I'd lost the will to fight them.

"Did he ever hit you?"

I nodded. "Playing ball kept me out of that house. It pushed me to be better, to be different, so I could escape. But I should've been there. If I hadn't run or hidden or whatever I was doing ..."

He waited, but words wouldn't come.

"Where are they now? Your parents?"

"They're dead," I mumbled. "She ... When I was eight, she took a butcher knife into the bathroom. The tub was so full, and steam poured out like there was a fire."

"You were there?"

"I found her."

"Oh, Nick. I am so sorry." His hands rose to my shoulders, and he pulled my head into his chest.

Then the sobs came.

I don't know how long we sat like that, how long he held me. I told him, in broken words, through a torrent of tears, how my father turned his anger toward me, blamed me for what she'd done, how she'd *left him*.

"He made himself a victim, then made me one."

Another eternity passed with André wrapped around me, sheltering me from the world, from my memories. I'd never told anyone about my parents. When I thought back, I'd never had any friends close enough to tell something like that. Maybe I hadn't let anyone close enough ...

I sat back and pulled the sheet to my eyes, wishing memories wiped like tears.

"What about your father?"

My hands froze, the sheet still covering my face. André waited.

"He answered a call—domestic abuse, if you can believe it. The husband was tearing into his wife with his belt. When Frank got there, the man pulled a gun and shot him, then his wife, then turned it on himself."

"My god."

"I didn't shed a single tear for him, André. Even now, I feel guilty for ... for feeling grateful to that man and his gun. I'm fucking evil, I know it."

"Nick, stop."

"I am! I'm glad he's dead. He deserved it."

"Nick, look at me. Just look at me."

I let my eyes drift up to find his gaze stern. There was no judgment or anger, just strength.

"What you feel is natural; normal, even. After what you saw, what you lived through, how could you not harbor anger toward your ... toward that man? I'm not judging or blaming you, not even a little."

I stared into him and found no lie.

"Really?"

"Yes, really. You are *nothing* like those men, either of them."

I drew in a deep breath and held it. Anger, pain, resentment, and grief welled up inside me, feelings I'd thought long buried now clawing their way to the fore. So many memories I'd hoped forgotten ...

"Where did you go when Frank died?"

I cocked my head.

"You were sixteen. Who did you live with?"

"Oh, I had an uncle and aunt who lived a few blocks over. They took me in."

"So you do have family?"

"No. They died a few years ago, killed in a car crash. They were the last of us ... except for me."

André reached forward and pulled my head against his, forehead to forehead.

"I'm sorry I unloaded on you like that," I whispered.

He pulled back and waited for me to look at him. "No, Nick, thank you for telling me. It takes great strength to reach out your hand. I admire you even more for doing so."

Had I reached out my hand? When had that happened?

I glanced around at the discarded comforter and sheets, at the pillows askew. For the first time all morning, I felt naked.

"I can't believe we just sat here, on the bed, talking about—"André lifted my chin. "I told you I would do whatever it took to get you out of your jeans, and here you are."

It felt good to laugh.

André's tenor and my bass sang freely. The more I tried to stop, the more flowed out. Before we knew it, we were both laying on our backs, howling at the ceiling. It felt like a dam had burst, and all the water it held was flooding my whole world. Or maybe it was washing away my pain?

My breaths grew deeper, flowed freer, as if André had unbuckled a strap that had constrained my chest for longer than I could remember. It wasn't gone—I still felt its metal digging into my soul—but the pressure had eased a bit.

"What would you like to do today, other than see Ethan?" he asked after my breathing finally returned to normal.

I smiled weakly and said, in my best big boy voice, "I'm hungry."

He grinned. "That we can fix."

We'd taken our time getting cleaned up and dressed, then sipped coffee and chatted with contented disregard for time. I was glad to be out of the apartment and away from memories and talk of them, and it was nearly noon by the time we finished a lazy brunch.

André swiped his badge at the gate and we made our way to one of the smaller buildings in the complex, one I hadn't visited before.

"We're not going to the rec center?" I asked.

"No. I'm taking you to the admin office." He pointed toward a building that resembled a ranch-style mini-mansion rather than the heart of an institution. I glanced around and realized, for the first time, that the whole place looked like one sprawling apartment complex. Each unit resembled the others, but not in a cold, institutional way. They looked like any multi-family home one might see in a residential neighborhood. They looked like *my* apartment complex.

I nodded, absently staring out the window at a cardinal that'd just landed nearby.

André put the car in park, reached over and squeezed my hand. "I'm not sure where Ethan will be at this time on a Sunday. We'll get you signed in and ask the desk where we can find him."

He led us in past a reception desk, where a portly woman of unguessable age smiled. "Hey, Doc. What brings you in on a weekend?"

André returned her smile. "Good morning, Janice. I am bringing Ethan a special guest."

Janice turned her raptor's gaze on me, and I suddenly felt like ducking below her counter or behind André for protection.

"Oh, hello there," she said. I'd read her gaze entirely wrong. "Aren't you just a delicious daiquiri on a summer's day?"

Heat flared through my body, and I felt my face turn redder than the cardinal's breast.

Janice cackled. "André, you brought me a frightened little rabbit. Should I pounce?"

André, the traitorous bastard, replied, "If you can catch him, you can have him. But he's more of a margarita than a daiquiri. I know how you enjoy a big worm in your tequila."

Janice howled. "And you know how I like a salty rim."

André practically pissed himself right there in the lobby.

My ears blazed and I slunk back, desperately searching for the exits I knew I wouldn't use.

André's hand found mine and he lifted it to his lips. "No, Janice, this concoction, whatever he may be, is not for sharing. Sorry to disappoint."

Her eyes widened, then her smile bloomed. "André, really? It's been years—"

"Yes, it has." He cut her off a little too abruptly, and I wasn't too embarrassed to notice. "This is Nick Dunlap. He is one of the Clippers who visits the children. He has been a great help with Ethan, and has become ... special to me as well."

Janice put both hands over her ample bosom. "It's nice to meet you, Nick. Just ignore all our teasing. We only pick on the ones we like, and I can tell Doc is smitten."

"Janice," André's tone warned.

"Oh, hush, you." She waved a hand at André like she was swatting a fly. "I can see it, plain as day, and it's beautiful. You're a good man, Doc. You deserve to be happy too."

"Well, thank you," he said, clearly uncomfortable with her praise.

"Alright, Mr. Nick, let's get you signed in so the big bad doc can take you to see the children."

I chuckled. Janice was growing on me.

"Ethan's in a group activity for the next forty minutes," she said, scanning a calendar on her computer. She clicked a few keys, then glanced up. "He's in B2. You can wait over there, but the common room might be more comfortable, maybe the staff lounge."

"Thanks, Janice. You are a diamond," André said.

She giggled and clutched her chest again. "You better take that hot young thing outta here before I eat you both up."

"*Oui, madame*," André said, and she swooned so hard I thought she might tip her chair backward.

André grabbed my hand and pulled me out of her reach. "She's right about being more comfortable. Forty minutes is a long time to sit in a metal folding chair outside a meeting room. Let's go back to the common room and get some coffee."

The moment we entered the large, familiar space, my Spidey sense tingled. I glanced around, trying to find whatever had set off my sixth sense, but there wasn't anyone around.

Then I spotted Noah slouched in the far corner staring out the window, exactly as I'd seen him that first day. André chatted loudly, unaware we had company, but Noah didn't turn or look up. I didn't get the impression he was looking at anything, more lost in thought.

I gave André's hand a squeeze. "Is it okay if I go say hi to Noah?"

André halted and scanned the room, finally landing on the troublesome teen. He stared silently for a long moment, then nodded slowly. "I suppose it couldn't hurt. Just ... never mind. Go say hi."

Well, that sounded ominous. I eyed André a second, then made my way across the room.

"Hey, Noah," I said when I was within a dozen or so paces.

He raised a middle finger in greeting.

"Dude, really?" I said, pulling a chair over and dropping down next to him. "Save that for the staff. Besides, I didn't know you were into birds. Is that what you're watching over here?"

He snorted, but his lips didn't curl or part.

"Just thought I'd say hi while I'm here. We're waiting to see Ethan."

"Yeah, figured," he huffed.

This was going well.

"So, what's been going on? How've you been?"

"Did Doc send you over here? It's the kind of sneaky shit they do, you know."

I crossed my arms. "No, I asked him if it was okay to come say hi. That's all. Why?"

"Why what?"

"Why do you think he would do that? Send me over to talk with you?" He scratched his head, then flicked his fingers like he'd picked something up for his effort. "I broke out, had myself a little day trip. Got everybody here all worked up, calling the cops and shit. Now they're all over me. I just figured—"

"That I was part of all that? No, I'm not. I didn't even know about it until now. I really did just want to say hi."

He finally turned from the window and regarded me, his eyes with a tempest of swells battering a rocky shore. I didn't think I'd ever seen a boy so troubled until that moment.

"What the fuck is it to you? Why do you care?"

I shrugged. "I don't know. Maybe I don't. Maybe I was just bored sitting here waiting, and you gave me an excuse to do something other than drink coffee with a shrink."

He glanced over my shoulder, across the room at André. "He babysitting you too?"

I grinned. "Something like that."

Then he dragged his feet off the window sill and leaned forward with his elbows on his knees. "You really a Clipper?"

"Yeah."

"You drive a Ferrari or something?"

I snorted, unable to hold back. "The Clippers are a minor league team. They probably pay the folks working in the cafeteria here more than me."

He grimaced. "No way."

"Sad, but true. We're a step above college kids and ramen noodles, but it's a really short step."

He almost smiled. Almost.

"Fuckin' sucks," he said. "You any good? Gonna make it onto a real team?"

I shrugged, ignoring the slight on the minor leagues. "I'm okay, and yeah, I'll get called up, get my name on an MLB jersey."

"Bet we don't see you here when that happens," he said, leaning back, slamming his sneakers back on the sill, resuming his staring match with the trees outside.

"Maybe. I don't know how all that would work, but I like coming here."

He scoffed. "Why the fuck would you like it here? All I want is to get out of this place."

I thought a moment. "I like seeing Ethan. He's a good kid, but I think he's lonely. If me coming here makes him feel a little less alone, then I want to give that to him."

Noah turned and stared. His gaze was so intense, I thought he might bore a hole through my chest. Then he turned back and fixed on some point beyond the fence. The silence stretched, but he didn't move. I wanted to ask him something, anything, just to get him to talk, but had no clue how to crack a petrified stone.

"Well, guess I'll grab that coffee now. I, uh ... thanks for talking."

André watched me rise and turn from Noah, watched me saunter across the room with slumped shoulders, like a player who'd just struck out for the third time. When I reached him, he didn't say a word, simply glanced over me to Noah, then smiled.

"Why are you smiling?" I grabbed a Styrofoam cup and dumped a couple creamers in.

"Because Noah watched you walk away."

Coffee streamed from the spout. "And that's a good thing because ...? He didn't throw a knife or anything, right?"

"Not yet. He still might." André grinned. "He wouldn't have watched you if something you said hadn't registered. However it might have felt, you reached him."

I groaned. "You're kidding, right? That guy's shell is thicker than the bricks on this building."

He nodded. "True, but with the right tools, even those bricks may break open."

I wanted to believe him, to know I'd done something good, but nothing about the conversation—if you could call it that—felt good, or even not so bad. It felt exactly like Noah would describe it: shitty.

Thankfully, my rumination was shattered by a high-pitched screech from the entrance.

"Nick!"

I turned just in time to save my coffee as Ethan slammed into me, his twig-like arms gripping me as tightly as they could muster. André grabbed my cup so I could reach down and return the boy's embrace.

"I missed you, kiddo."

He squeezed harder. "I really missed you too. You're still my best friend, right?"

I grabbed his knobby head in both hands and pulled him back. "Best friend ever."

He didn't look convinced. "You promise?"

"On my honor as a Clipper."

For some ridiculous reason known only to eight-year-olds, that lit up his face like a freshly decked Christmas tree.

I glanced up to catch André smothering his mouth with a hand while wiping an eye with his other.

"Big softie," I muttered.

André lowered his hands and a smile unfurled. His eyes shifted upward, so I followed his gaze.

Noah was watching.

Twenty-Five

André

It's funny how time moves differently at moments in our lives. The weeks that followed our Mexican restaurant adventure were a blur for me. The Ranch took in far too many children at once, a byproduct of the closure of another local facility due to state budget cuts. Every surviving home in the area was bulging beyond capacity. The nerves of countless doctors and staff were frayed. I worked twelve, sometimes fourteen-hour days, something I hadn't done since the early days of my career.

But those who truly suffered through the shortage were the children. They were vulnerable, hurting, and alone. They needed us, far more of us than we could give.

Over those same weeks, Nick's clock slowed.

For most players, the off-season was a time for family, vacations, travel, and anything else that might be a fun relief from the grueling one-hundred-sixty-plus-game slog of the season. Nick had no family. He didn't really have many friends, other than Zack and Kervin. He was in a new city, living in a new apartment, driving his new car, with no work or school or anything to keep him occupied.

All he had in abundance was time.

Being the Nick I'd come to care for, he chose to give that one precious commodity away. Every day, around noon, after his morning workout, Nick arrived at the gate bearing a cooler filled with sandwiches, baked chicken, or whatever concoction he'd dreamed up for us. We'd eat lunch in my office, then he'd wander down to the common room to spend his afternoons with Ethan.

The change I witnessed in that boy was nothing short of a miracle. As elated as we had been when he'd spoken again, our joy was redoubled as we witnessed him emerge from his shell a fully formed, beautifully happy child. He still struggled to sleep, troubled by dreams we spent hours discussing, but he smiled. He laughed. He played with Nick, and eventually the other children near his age, something he hadn't done since his first days with us.

He was still categorized as unadoptable. It would take far more time to remove that sticker from his file, but he had erased all of the high-risk flags that worried us so.

Seeing him with Nick was unlike anything I'd experienced. On a professional level, I was fascinated to watch Ethan's transformation. He'd clearly bonded with Nick, but their relationship was far more complex than volunteer and patient. It wasn't just Ethan who looked at Nick differently than he did anyone else. Nick's eyes *changed* when Ethan entered the room. They widened and brightened. They filled with awe. They smiled.

I knew those shifts, those emotional tells, from my training, my years of experience, and, if I was honest with myself, from something far deeper within. They were the same changes *my* eyes made every day around noon when he appeared at the gate.

Like some squatter hanging drapes in the house he inhabited, Nick had moved into my heart, unbidden, and wholly claimed me for his own. As much as the difference in our ages frightened me, it was clear the mystical, magnetic pull that slammed our lives together was stronger than any resistance either of us might offer.

And, honestly, I didn't want to offer any.

He spent more nights in my bed than in his own, only returning when laundry piled up or his pantry needed refilling. Just thinking about us in bed, I could feel his skin pressing against mine, his heat warming my soul. It made my skin prickle in the most sensual way, like someone had just run fingernails gently over it, tickling and teasing. It made me ache for his touch.

More than a month had passed, and we had explored each other like shipwrecked sailors fumbling across a new land. He was tender and sweet, then passionate and rough, then vulnerable and shy. He let me see the small boy, still unsure and afraid. He let me hold him, soothe him, give him strength. In every way but one, he gave himself to me, and I was sure the day would come, hopefully not too far away, when I would feel him give that to me as well.

My body yearned for that. It had been so long.

I watched him unwrap his lunch, such a simple, unassuming act. How did he make it look so sexy? The stubborn lock, his forever nemesis, bobbed across his forehead. Even that was hot—*especially* that.

The arrogant, self-absorbed, plastic pro player I'd dreamed up turned out to be the most humble, selfless, deeply layered man I'd met in years. Every time I thought I knew the real Nick, he would say or do something, reveal some tidbit from his past that made me see him with fresh eyes.

Part of me fought the weightless feeling as I fell helplessly into his arms. Out of control barely described it. The mention of his name sent my blood flowing faster. Seeing a text or call from him—or worse, watching him walk up the drive toward the building each day—turned my heart into some reckless teen who refused to be tamed.

It felt incredible.

And terrifying.

He had no distractions, no practice or games. There weren't adoring fans clogging his social media, or other players claiming his free time. When spring came and his uniform fell across his shoulders once more, would everything change? Would he see me for the middle-aged, past-his-prime man I was?

I tried to be the patient in my own mind, offering counseling and advice to the inner child who thrashed so violently in my chest, but objectivity was impossible within one's own orbit. The planets would spin and arc, but never align.

So, I was left with the flimsy thread, the thinnest of strands that was hope.

My heart hoped he would stay. It hoped I was enough.

"Do you think Dr. Marber would let me take Ethan off-campus sometime?" Nick asked through bites of tuna salad sandwich.

I swallowed, then took a sip of tea. "What did you have in mind?"

"Well, I was thinking," he said, with a hint of pride. "Maybe I could take him to the stadium, let him play catch with a pro baller on a real pro field?"

The image of Nick and Ethan tossing a baseball on the Clippers' grassy outfield made me smile. "I'll talk with her, but expect she will want anything like that supervised by either Sara or me. There are legal liabilities involved."

He nodded. "I get it. Sara would probably enjoy a day at the park."

My desk chair screamed as I leaned back, expressing exactly what I felt. "Sara?"

He smirked. "Or you, I guess, if I was stuck with you that day."

I tossed a wadded napkin at him, and he laughed.

"Is that how you treat patients who annoy you? You throw things at them? There must be some rule about abuse."

"Oh, stop, or I'll ..." I glanced around, desperate to find something larger to toss. "I'll—"

Whatever I was going to say died as Nick rose, leaned over my desk, and kissed me.

"There's no one in the world I'd rather go to the park with than you and Ethan," he whispered, his breath tickling my still-moist lips.

"I, uh, will talk with ... her ... Dr. Marber." I'd turned into a babbling fool over one kiss.

He gave me another peck, then sat back. "Awesome. I won't say anything to E until it's approved. Last thing I want to do is get the little guy's hopes up and then be told we can't go."

I cocked my head. "E?"

"Every player needs a nickname. He's too young for our usual tags, so I went with something simple. He seems to like it."

I shook my head. Those two were something.

"Nick, I have been meaning to ask you something." I glanced down at my hands, gathering my thoughts. "Holidays are difficult for many of our children. They are reminders of traditions they do not enjoy, families they no longer have. We do our best to make those days feel special, but that means I am here, working."

"Yes," he said.

"I have not asked a question."

He grinned. "I know you, Frenchie. You're going to ask something, but you have to give me a thousand reasons for asking before you do. It's adorable, but takes *so* much time."

I quirked a brow. "Alright. What are you agreeing to do?"

"To have Thanksgiving here, with you and the kids, of course. Why else would you bring up holidays a week before Turkey Day?"

"He's not just pretty, but smart too."

The napkin I'd tossed smacked into my chest and fell to my lap.

"Thank you, Nick. It will mean the world to the children. And to me."

"No need to get all mushy. I know I'm amazing," he said, doing a dramatic model hair-flick to punctuate his point. "Alright, I'll let you get back to work. We have trucks to race today."

Ethan's birthday was still six months away, but Nick had insisted on getting him a half-year present, a tradition with which I was wholly unfamiliar and suspected had been made up on the spot. The present for this auspicious holiday was a set of Hot Wheels trucks that fit with Ethan's obsession du jour.

"Have fun, and would you please let the boy win?" I grinned.

"Never. He has to learn to win on his own. Can't have my kiddo grow up spoiled," he said before closing the door behind me.

I steepled my fingers, replaying his words. *His* kiddo. I couldn't decide if that thrilled or troubled me more.

Twenty-Six

Nick

My room finally looked like someone lived in it. I'd spent most of the morning cobbling together items I'd bought at Target and a few local shops. My meager budget—and even more pitiful skill with anything artistic—didn't allow for much in the way of decorating, but I had to make the place my own. I could feel judgment in André's eyes every time he slept over. He'd stare at the barren bed with its threadbare sheets and wafer-thin comforter, then try not to glare at walls that'd not seen a painting or picture in years.

Adoring doctor aside, I needed it to feel homey, like I belonged here. The move from Nashville had been so sudden, so unexpected. Then, before I really knew what was happening, the season ended and most of my teammates had vanished. Making this place my own personal retreat was important, so I spent a few bucks to make it feel that way.

The last thing to adorn my walls was, without doubt, the most meaningful—and it hadn't cost a penny. Ethan had made me a drawing of the two of us playing ball on the lawn at the Ranch. His representation of me looked more like a superhero than a baseball player. I loved it, even if André scoffed at how the child was "bloating my ego." It was a little disturbing that Ethan had included the fencing that surrounded the compound in his drawing, but I supposed that was his reality.

The drawing went above my nightstand where I would see it each night before going to sleep. A kid's stick-drawing didn't exactly go with my pro player motif, but it was perfect in every way. As I was straightening the now-framed Picasso, my phone chimed. I glanced down and grinned at the name on the screen.

> **MyRoomie:** Hello, Nick. How is the Thanksgiving going?

Marcus's English wasn't exactly broken. It was better than that description, but it was very clearly stretched, possibly torn in places, and I loved every bit of it.

> **Me:** The Thanksgiving is next week and should be fun. We're all going to the Ranch for the day. What about you?

> **MyRoomie:** Thanksgiving is an American tradition. Here, there is sun, the ocean, beautiful women. Every day in Brazil we are thankful.

> **Me:** That all sounds great, but you miss me. I can tell.

> **MyRoomie:** Really, you can tell?

> **Me:** Oh yes. I can picture you laying around in your boxers, possibly diddling yourself, wishing I was there to help you.

MyRoomie: I missed you until then. I am good to diddle without a man.

Me: Oh, I am too, but it's always better with one. A double diddle. Two guys, two diddles. What could be more festive?

We'd exchanged a number of texts since he'd left for home, each becoming more familiar, teasing, and utterly irreverent. From the brief time we'd hung out in person, and from what Zack and Kervin had told me, Marcus was as gay-friendly as a guy could be without actually sucking cock himself, and I couldn't help but wonder …

He and I had talked a few times about André, mostly over text. He didn't like talking on the phone, and neither of us wanted to pay international rates. On paper, I hardly knew him, but my gut trusted him implicitly, and that was good enough. For whatever reason, we just clicked, and I had a feeling we would be best friends, a dynamic duo, when he returned to the States. The Clippers wouldn't know what hit them.

MyRoomie: I will think on your diddling, but only while I am not diddling. I would rather my diddler not become confused.

Me: So, you're saying there's a chance your diddler might like to be diddled?

MyRoomie: I am beginning to wonder why I texted you, you fucking diddler.

Me: Listen, you diddling twat. Wait, that should be twat diddler. That's what you do, right?

MyRoomie: If a twat enjoys diddling by a tall, very handsome Brazilian, of course.

Me: Eww. All of that. Just eww.

MyRoomie: You do not think I am handsome?

I had to change the conversation before I said something I actually meant.

Me: It will be nice when you come back. You can meet André, and Ethan will love you.

MyRoomie: Ethan is the boy? And André is the man you diddle?

Me: Yes, Ethan is the boy. André and I have only diddled so far.

There was a pause, then the dots began to dance.

MyRoomie: Are you afraid to diddle all the way with this André?

Me: No, I'm not afraid.

MyRoomie: You have been seeing him how long?

Me: Since you left. Two months, as of this week.

MyRoomie: Two months? And you have not done the Big Diddle?

MyRoomie: Nick, is your diddler broken? Do you have diddle drip? There is a cream for that, or a pill, I am not sure. My diddler has never dripped.

Me: No! My diddler is just fine. André and I even got tested, just to be sure everything is good.

MyRoomie: Then why no pokey with the diddler?

Was this conversation happening between two grown men or kids leafing through their first *Playboy* magazine?

> **Me:** At first I wanted to wait. I really like this guy, Marcus. I mean, I think I'm falling pretty hard here.

> **Me:** After that, I'm not sure. He's working like crazy and I just didn't want to push things. They've been going so great. I didn't want to blow it.

> **MyRoomie:** Blowing it leads to diddling.

> **Me:** LOL you are an idiot. Stop making me laugh.

> **MyRoomie:** Seriously, are you ready to take the next step with him?

> **Me:** I can't stop thinking about him. When we're not together, I'm crawling the walls.

> **MyRoomie:** Please do not scratch the walls. They will keep my deposit.

Me: Asshole!

MyRoomie: My asshole is beautiful, but do not get ideas. It is not for diddling.

Me: Fuck me.

MyRoomie: Asking politely will not change things, but I applaud your effort.

Me: OMG!

MyRoomie: I have to go now. The family is gathering for a meal. My mother would be very unhappy if I became late. She swings a very large ladle.

Me: I don't need to know about your mother's ladle. That's disgusting.

MyRoomie: Leaving you now.

Me: Miss you too. Hugs and kisses.

Twenty-Seven

Nick

"You're just going to have to wait. If I pull this out of the oven now, we'll poison the poor kids." Zack flew around the kitchen like Julia Child on crack. His voice was nearly as high-pitched, jumping an octave with each passing quarter-hour.

"I just don't know how you expected me to get all this done in such a short time. I have three trays of different vegetables, two sheet pans of cornbread, and two whole turkeys. Oh, and four pans of dressing. Who cooks four pans of dressing? Are you trying to kill me here?"

Kervin and I stayed far away, on the opposite side of their swirly table, chuckling quietly.

"Is he always like this in the kitchen?" I asked.

"Nope," he whispered. "I think knowing a few dozen kids will judge his food has him worked up. I just hope he keeps his hair away from the stove. That shit would go up like kindling."

I grunted. Zack's hair was even larger than normal. If he hadn't been the whitest man ever born, I would've thought it was an impressive afro, albeit brown. Women all over America would sacrifice small children to have his curls.

"Should we, I don't know, help him?"

Kervin shot me a glare. "Hell no. You want to get in the middle of that, go right ahead. I'm staying over here, where it's safe and there are no knives."

We watched in silence as someone in the clouds pressed the fast-forward button, and the Zack Show flipped into high gear. There was nothing on the stove; it was all in the oven. There was nothing to do but wait for food to cook. I couldn't figure out what he was running around for, but it was hilarious, so we sat and watched.

"So," Kervin whispered, afraid a raised voice might catch the ire of the fuzzy-headed Iron Chef. "What are we walking into today?"

Was he asking about the meal with the kids, or André? The first was easy; the second, I hadn't even asked myself, much less answered.

Zack and Kervin were the perfect couple, a match made in gay heaven. Defining their relationship was easy—at least, from the outside looking in, it was crystal clear. André and I had yet to label whatever we were. Neither of us had used the "boyfriend" term. Hell, we hadn't used any term to describe us. I'd only ever dated one guy for longer than a month, and that was a college fling that flopped. The terms were still so confusing to me.

I'd known André for two and a half months. We started dating a week after we met, give or take a few days of him hating me. Was that long enough to call us a couple? Were we boyfriends? Did the fact we'd still not done the big nasty affect our status as a couple?

And then there was the L word. I'd never used that about anyone other than my mom. My dad was too reprehensible, so he never heard that word from my lips. Since they died, I couldn't remember a single time I'd said it to anyone.

Wasn't that a sad thing to realize?

"Dude, it wasn't a hard question. Why do you look like you're passing a turd the size of Kansas?"

A chuckle offered much-needed relief from my mental gymnastics.

"It's just a big meal with lots of kids. That's all. They'll probably do something fun, like a Thanksgiving play. André didn't tell me all the details."

He was silent a moment, then asked, "What's with you and André? Every time you say his name, you get this look in your eyes."

"What look?" I asked, not meaning to sound defensive.

"Like you're about to turn into a Disney chipmunk and break into song. Do you love this guy or what?"

Shit.

There it was. The L word again.

Kervin said it so easily, like it was the most obvious thing in the world, like I should just know if I loved someone or not. Why did people think love was obvious when it was the most elusive, ill-defined, mutable emotion ever conceived? All I really knew about love was that my dad said it when he wanted to apologize for ... things I'd feel for weeks. If *that* was love, I didn't want anything to do with it.

My mom's love, what I remembered of it, was pure. I could still remember her eyes, just barely, as they stared down at me. They were stars in the heaven, guiding me to safety, stealing away the darkness of night. Her hand on my cheek was a balm to my soul and eased every pain. Was that love? It had to be a mother's love, but did couples feel that way about each other too? Was that feeling only reserved for a mother and child?

Then I thought about my time with André, how he held me, how *he* cupped my cheek. It was one of his favorite gestures. I tried to picture him in my mind, reaching out, tried to feel his warmth as it pressed to my skin. My heart bloomed at his touch. I felt safe and whole. I felt at home.

Was that love?

"I ... I don't know. I think, maybe, I might. A little." I wanted the answer. I wanted to tell Kervin, to shout it, to scream it louder than anyone ever screamed, but I still wasn't sure. I still didn't *know*. It felt like a wild, reckless guess of an answer, a gamble with no chips left, putting everything I had, everything I was, on the line.

Why did one word feel like that?

His brows knitted, then smoothed. "Okay. I'll let you get away with a lame answer like that—for now."

I didn't laugh or chuckle or grunt. I didn't turn to face him. I just stared at Zack, not really seeing him.

"How did you know you loved him?"

The sound of serving dishes and metal spoons clanking against granite filled the kitchen.

"He said it on, like, our third date. I nearly walked out right then." I could see Kervin smiling out the corner of my eye. "Then, a few weeks later, we went to this house party. One of our friends had a birthday and wanted every gay man within a hundred miles to know it. His house was packed, and the men were insanely hot—like, Marcus hot—but all gay."

"Damn."

"Yeah, but that's my point. We didn't ride together. I had to do something—I don't even remember what now—and we'd agree to meet at the party. I walked in after most of the guys had already arrived. Music was blaring. Some of them were dancing without their shirts. Sweat and muscles were everywhere.

"When I finally found Zack, all those men faded into the background. It was like somebody hit a switch and everyone but us was fuzzed out or turned gray. We were the only ones in full color. *He* was the only one I saw. I knew, right there, in the middle of that party, that I could never spend a day without him. So I wove through the crowd, grabbed him by the shoulders, and greeted him with, 'I love you, Zack,' right there in front of everybody."

"Wow. And you call *me* a Disney character."

He snickered. "Yeah, guys around us applauded as we kissed. That's all I remember of them. There was only Zack. There will only ever be Zack." His voice took on a distant tenor as he stared at his man across the room.

God, was love always that intense?

While touching, their story only added pressure to my uncertainty. I didn't know if André was some magical being from another world sent here to fill my soul with unicorn dust ... or something. That's how realistic Zack and Kervin's tale sounded to me. Unicorn dust, or farts, or turds. Love is turds.

That made me laugh.

"Dude, I tell you the most heartwarming thing ever said, and you laugh?"

"Sorry," I said through stifled giggles. "It wasn't you. I was ... never mind."

'Fearless' by Taylor Swift blared from Zack's iPhone.

"Alright, besties, food's ready. Time to pack the car," he proclaimed.

"Taylor is his alarm ring? Really?" I whispered to Kervin.

He grinned and shrugged. "She's the only person he'd leave me for. You know how those Swifties are."

We walked into the Ranch common room and were greeted by a wall of sound. Laughter, screams, and a few squeals from raucous children filled our ears, while mouthwatering aromas made my stomach do backflips. While the children played, staff scurried about, laden with trays of savory delights drawn from carts freshly wheeled from the kitchen.

Several rows of folding tables had been erected along the center. Plastic tablecloths covered in orange-and-brown cartoon images depicted vegetables with arms, legs, and googly eyes dancing with turkeys and deer. Another series of tables pressed against the walls created a serving area that spanned nearly half the room.

"Why did I cook so much food? It looks like they made enough for the whole city," Zack said, as we hauled the first load of homemade goodness toward the table where Janice held court. She appeared to be directing traffic, ensuring every plate, fork, and tray found its proper home.

"Trust me, the kids will crush your food. The kitchen here does okay, but it's not the same."

"Somebody sure knows a lot about this place, even knows how the food tastes," Kervin said, eyeing me with a sly grin.

Before I could respond, a human torpedo slammed into me. "Nick! Did you see all the food? And there's so many desserts. Like cherry pie, apple pie, cobbler, brownies, candy. There's everything! I'm gonna eat it all."

Ethan released me long enough for me to muss his hair then darted away. I caught a quick glimpse of a tiny truck in one of his hands.

"That's why I know so much. I have my own personal tour guide," I said to my two gaping friends. "Come on. Let's get all your food set up so we can hang out with the kids."

Janice pounced the moment we stepped back inside. She pointed for Zack to go one direction, while spinning Kervin in another, and barking orders for me to deliver my platters to the table at the front of the room. Everything had its place, and she clearly wouldn't allow anyone, guest or not, to muddy her system.

I set my dish down and turned back to watch the kids. As I scanned the room, something on the far side caught my eye. André was leaning against the wall at the far end where we'd entered, but we'd been so intent on getting our food inside and settled, I hadn't noticed him.

Then he glanced up, our eyes met, and sunlight surged from his smile.

It was the strangest sensation.

The chorus of kids died away. Their running and dancing dimmed. Even the perpetual barking of Janice's orders faded to background noise.

All I saw was André.

He raised a hand and waved. My heart leapt into my throat as my own hand mirrored the gesture.

Why is the room so hot all of the sudden? I wondered, tugging at my collar, even though I wore a loose-fitting polo shirt whose collar was already fully open.

I took a step forward, then another, traversing the minefield of wriggling youngsters who barely drew my eye. The more steps I took, the faster my heart raced. It felt like walking through a dream, through a hazy fog of memories—only, it was real. André stood before me, only a few strides away.

His hair was pushed back, the waves flowing freely on each side. His thick-rimmed glasses framed his eyes, making him at once nerdy and intelligent in the most seductive way. My breath caught as I stood before him.

"André ... I ..."

"Hey, you," he said, his smile broadening beyond possibility.

"I love you," tumbled out, jarring me into the present. A cacophony of sound slammed into my ears, and frozen time leapt forward. Had I actually spoken? What had I said?

André stared, his mouth open, his eyes wide.

What the hell had I just said?

"I love you," flew out again. *Oh shit.* I covered my mouth with a hand to stop the demon from betraying me any further.

André reached up, pulled my hand away, and kissed me deeply.

My brain went limp, along with my legs.

Only when the children around us began chanting and jeering with shouts of, "Eww, kissing," and "Dr. André has a boyfriend," did we pull apart.

Still, André's eyes remained fixed on mine. Then he cupped my cheek, and my whole body turned to gel.

"I love you, Nick Dunlap. I love you so much."

Twenty-Eight

Nick

Zack and Kervin only gave me a little shit when I told them André wanted to take me home. Zack's teasing was relentless, but Kervin remained silent, his approval evident in his smiling eyes.

"Is it okay if I get my car tomorrow?" I asked.

Kervin wrapped me in his arms. "Idiot. Go get laid. Your car will be fine."

I gave him a peck on the cheek, then climbed into André's car.

"I didn't think that would ever end," André said as my door slammed shut.

"We *were* there for them, right?" I teased.

He shifted in his seat, reached over and grabbed my head, then kissed me like he was never going to see me again.

For the second time that night, all thought—and most of my breath—fled, and I became a puddle of mush in his hands. When he pulled back, I couldn't move. All I could do was stare at him, lost in the perfection of his lips and cheeks and eyes. Even his nose was perfect ... well, except for the forest of hair clawing out of it. My brain finally decided to intervene, flashing images of tiny monkeys swinging from his nose hair, one nostril to the other, then back.

That had to tickle.

I spat out a laugh.

"That was not the reaction a Frenchman hopes for from his kiss," he said, cocking an accusing brow.

I smothered his protest with my mouth. Monkeys be damned.

"Would you please take me home?"

He nodded, then turned and revved the engine.

We'd barely made it through his door when André turned and shoved me against the wall.

"You are mine. All mine," he growled. I'd seen him play aggressive before, but never actually *be* aggressive. Something in this shift sent a bolt down my spine, and made my cock stiffen.

"All yours," was all he let me say before smothering my mouth. His hands grabbed my wrists, pinning them out to the side, as his body slammed into me, nearly driving the breath from my lungs.

"I love you, Nick. Let me show you how much."

I moaned, craning my neck as his teeth grazed, then bit into my skin. His tongue followed, and I squirmed. I could feel how much he wanted me, his erection pressing into my own each time he shoved our bodies together.

This gentle man, this healer of minds and hearts, was a raging beast, and I was his prey. A tiny voice told me to hold back, to be afraid, but I slapped that bitch back into the fucking closet and gave myself completely to André. If he wanted to kiss, we'd kiss. If he wanted to fuck like animals, grunting and pounding, we'd be monsters.

"I want you inside me tonight," he said, and I thought my world might explode.

"I belong to you, André. Everything I have, everything I am, it's yours."

He pulled back at that, eyeing, assessing in that professorial way he had when one of his patients said something intriguing. Then something clicked in his eyes, and there were no more questions, no more requests or doubts or hesitations.

We left a trail of clothes, starting with my shirt at the front door and ending with our tangled underwear just outside the bedroom. Our journey across his house was an ungainly dance of arms, legs, lips, and cocks. Reaching, grasping, slamming together, until we finally reached his bed and he shoved me so I fell onto my back.

"*Mon dieu*. Your body is *magnifique*. I have seen it so many times, but still ..." he said, staring down.

I loved it when he slipped in and out of French. That's when I knew he was really out of his head and in the moment.

I reached up and pulled him by the hand onto the bed, then laid him down beside me on his back. My fingers traced around his nipples, swirling his hair into tiny silver whirlpools. He twitched at my touch, so I gripped him between my forefinger and thumb, and he groaned. His nipples were a gateway, and I intended to pass all the way through.

On my knees, I crawled to the foot of the bed and lifted his legs, kissing his feet as I did. His body tensed.

"Relax. I've got you."

He blew out a breath.

I knelt down and licked the head of his dick. He was so excited, slickness had dribbled down his shaft. I took him in my mouth and swirled my tongue, savoring every drop, then dove down so his full length filled my throat. He pulsed in my mouth, and I felt him shift and moan with each rise and fall.

I'd been so focused on sucking his cock that I'd nearly missed how my own dick rubbed between his cheeks, teasing his hole. I reached down and gently prodded with one finger.

"God, you're tight.""Uhh," came out, more moan than reply.

I wet my finger then slipped it back down, nudging the tip inside, while still riding his cock with my mouth and tongue.

His moan grew louder.

I eased my finger further in. Then further, then past the knuckle.

He clenched, then finally relaxed.

I slipped all the way inside him, pulling back long enough to slide in again. When he no longer resisted, a second finger joined the first.

"Fuck!" he called.

Both fingers pressed inside.

"Nick, dammit, get inside me. Please."

I sucked him faster, fucked him harder with my fingers.

He began to sweat.

And then I pulled my fingers out and sat upright, my cock twitching between his cheeks.

"There's lube in the nightstand," he said, pointing with a lifeless arm.

"Condom?" I asked.

He hesitated.

"André—" I said with a warning tone.

"We tested, Nick. We both tested. I've not been with anyone since we met."

I grunted. "I haven't been with anybody in years."

"Just get inside me, please," he said.

My rational brain was scolding me, but he was right. We had both tested negative, and I trusted that he'd not been with anyone since. I certainly hadn't.

So, I reached over and grabbed the lube.

Oily liquid drizzled into my palm, then over my cock. I reached down and slicked his hole, slipping two fingers back inside—easily this time. I added a third and thought André might leap off the bed.

"Sorry."

"There is no word for sorry in French. Do that again. Now!" he commanded.

So I did, harder this time. His body heaved. And again.

His eyes were closed. His hands gripped the sheets. His abs were tensed.

And that's when I slid inside him for the first time.

"Nick!" he yelled, a full-throated howl that was the hottest sound I'd ever heard.

I pulled back slowly, then pressed in again. His hands gripped my hips and held me there, as deep as I could get.

"No more gentle," he said.

I drew back and slammed into him as hard as I could. He bellowed. And again. And again. Our bodies found a rhythm as they collided over and over. He reached down to touch himself, but I slapped his hand away.

"Not a chance," I said, then grabbed him roughly and flipped him over, propping him up on his knees.

"Nick—"

I cut him off, slamming into him from behind so hard his body lurched forward. If I hadn't been holding his hips, he would've hit the headboard. Like the animals he begged us to be, I drove myself into him until we both blazed and dripped. His back arched, begging me to fill him deeper, thrust harder. My fingers dug into his flesh and pulled him toward me, willed me further, deeper, wholly inside him.

My body tensed, and I could feel the moment coming, so I pulled back—and out.

"What are you—"

I silenced him again, flipping him onto his back. "I want to see you, to kiss you, when it happens."

He reached up and cupped my cheek.

I slid back inside, my body now shivering at his touch.

"I won't last long now," I said, grasping his shaft and beginning to stroke.

"Make me yours, Nick. I want to give myself to you."

"You already are mine, André."

I leaned down and kissed him as I thrust. The beasts had fled at the sight of two men in love. Our mouths mingled, tongues pressed, and I slid slowly, fully, in and out.

"Oh shit, I'm—"

"Do it!" he said.

I pushed in, and my abs drew tight. I thought his ass grabbed me harder, but fire was flaring behind my eyes, and I couldn't think. A wave of ecstasy, like a tsunami, battered my body as the first of my elation released inside him. Still I pressed, pushing myself inside, emptying into him.

As the last of my shudders subsided, he cried out, his hole squeezed.

"Fuck, Nick!"

Wet heat shot out of him, coating his chest and my stomach. He twitched a few more times, then fell still.

"Don't pull out. Stay inside me, please."

I worked my way up so both our heads fell on a pillow, then wrapped my arms around him.

We fell asleep that way: two men, one heart.

Twenty-Nine

André

With the passing of Thanksgiving, December's holidays jumbled together in a mass of tinsel, tops, and trees. Nick's sleepovers went from overnight affairs to me clearing out drawers in both the bedroom and bathroom. He didn't fully move in, but I counted on one hand the number of times he slept in his apartment from Thanksgiving to New Year's Eve.

I knew our time together was a luxury soon to dwindle, and that likely drove us to spend every moment possible joined at the hip, figuratively and literally. If I had worried about my age limiting our physical activities, that had been for naught. If anything, his youthful exuberance had awakened my libido in ways I barely remembered from my youth. After that first night of unrepentant sex, we became ravenous, devouring each other every night, sometimes multiple times. Feeling him inside me, becoming one with him, filled my soul as much as ... other places. I didn't think I could get any happier.

Then one year passed and another rose.

We didn't go out to a bar or party. Zack and Kervin begged us to join them, but neither of us found that idea appealing, despite the fact we hung out with the guys several times each week. We'd become one large, crazy family. Still, there were some moments Nick and I jealously guarded. Celebration of the new year was one of them.

At the stroke of midnight, we stood before our television, dancing to the music, lips locked in celebration of far more than the turning of the calendar.

Little did I know, Nick would also turn that evening.

Turn over, to be precise.

A flash of panic and nerves washed over me as he lifted his legs, but when I slid inside him and saw his eyes, the last of my fears fled. I pressed inside him, held myself there, in that perfect space, and stared in wonder at the man who loved me. He stroked my hair, then ran his fingers along my arm. Still, I didn't move, joined in body and spirit.

When the moment shifted, and I began to thrust, his moans of pleasure urged me on. Sweat coated his smooth, chiseled body, abs glistening in the lamplight. My pulse quickened with every thrust. His moans became groans, then shouts. I pumped harder, slamming my cock inside him, rocking his body. He gripped my chest, kneaded the muscles, and dug at the skin. When I grabbed his cock and stroked, his hands flew to his legs as he stretched himself open even wider, willing me deeper.

"Nick, god, I'm close!"

"Fill me up, André. I want everything. I want you living inside me."

Those words, and the raging fire in his eyes, sent me over the edge, beyond all control or thought. My heart thundered. My body raged. My vision flared.

And we became one in every way.

I knew in that moment, this man was my world, and I would do anything to see him smile.

Winter wrestled with spring, but the baseball gods cared little for the seasons' battles. Spring training was inviolate, and the boys of summer flocked back to Columbus. We would all head to Goodyear, Arizona, the traditional home of our pre-season work, but everyone enjoyed a few weeks reunited before baseball consumed our lives again.

The week before we left for Arizona, Nick invited Marcus to my house for dinner. His roommate had just returned from Brazil, and neither of us wanted his first night back to be spent alone, scrounging for crumbs in their barren apartment. I knew, from Nick's description, that Marcus was tall and handsome. I hadn't expected the Latin Henry Cavill to swagger through our door. I reached out a hand in the favored greeting of most Americans, only to have it swept aside as the meaty giant pulled me into a muscly embrace. I couldn't decide whether to struggle for breath or surrender to a pleasant death.

All Nick said, as Marcus excused himself to the restroom, was, "Told you." His amused grin said everything else.

I prepared coq au vin, sure my doubling of the recipe would satisfy my men and leave me plenty for the week's lunches. Marcus proved as large an eater as he was a man, practically licking the pans once the chicken was gone.

After dinner, we drank wine and listened to Marcus tell of his time in South America. He spoke of his ever-growing family, thanks to the birth of a nephew. It was beautiful to watch the brawny man melt as he recalled holding the infant for the first time. I imagined the baby might have been smaller than his biceps when cradled in those arms.

As the evening wound down, Marcus helped carry Nick's suitcase and larger items and load them into his car. Nick left his toothbrush and a few changes of clothes at my place, but moved most of his things back into his apartment. I could tell his heart was torn, but his mind knew he needed to be closer to the stadium, closer to his team.

And while I knew he wasn't leaving, it still felt like the turning of a page. Things would never be the same—as if anything *ever* remained the same.

My heart ached at the emptiness of his drawers after he drove away. I held his shirt to my face, breathing in his scent, willing him to fill my house and heart—but I knew that was silly. He filled my heart no matter where he laid his head at night.

Still ...

The first of March was a Monday. I'd worked over the weekend, supervising a special event for our younger children, so I had the day off. My brain refused to sleep in, so I sat at my kitchen table, steaming mug in hand, as the sun peeked over the horizon.

I loved sunrise. Each one was a birth, a beginning, something fresh and new.

Nick had volunteered to attend Pitchers' Camp the prior week, along with the team's rookies, earning even more good grace with his new coaching staff. Between workouts, multiple practices, and teambuilding events, he would be consumed with spring training.

I sipped coffee, savoring the rich, French vanilla creamer sweetening the bitter beans. As I set the mug on the table, my phone rang.

The clock above the refrigerator read five thirty-five.

I groaned, dreading whatever emergency had occurred at work.

"This is Dr. Martin."

"Hey, you," Nick said.

A grin curled my lips.

"Aren't you up early?"

"Yeah. Sucks. On top of that, I forgot to get coffee when I moved back." His voice sounded like that kid fighting his mom as she dragged him out of bed for school. "I just wanted to hear your voice before all this starts."

"That is a perfect reason to call. I was just sipping coffee and watching the sunrise."

"Thanks for rubbing in the coffee thing," he griped.

"Should I bring you coffee? Is this a caffeine emergency?"

He smothered the phone and called out, "Be right there. Almost done." Then his voice returned to full volume. "Gotta go. Tell Ethan I'm wearing the bracelet he made me."

My heart soared. "Of course. Have a good first day. I love you."

"I love you too. Miss you already."

The line clicked to silence, leaving me staring at a blank screen as his name faded to black.

Spring training was rough.

The team indeed practiced twice each day, and mandatory morning workouts had the men up early, pushing each other to their limits in the weight room.

Nick and I didn't see each other all week.

We called and texted, and those interactions, however brief, were a precious respite from my lonely longing.

It was likely silly, me missing him so, but we had come to spend most of our time together, and his sudden absence from my daily routine left me adrift in my free time. Ethan was pitiful, in the way only a child could be. I took a cue from Nick's time with him, bought a glove, and brought a change of clothes each day so we could play catch in the afternoon sun. I wasn't uncoordinated, but I had never played America's pastime.

Ethan became my coach.

On the Sunday following the final day of spring training, Nick surprised me by showing up on my doorstep at seven in the morning.

"Hey, you," I said, opening the door. He had a key, but still knocked and waited to be admitted.

He stepped in and planted a kiss on my lips, then handed me a bundle of scarlet and violet lilies. He'd never brought me flowers.

"Nick, these are beautiful. What is the occasion?"

Pride—and a bit of smugness—infused his smile.

"Two occasions," he said, holding up two fingers. "First, I haven't seen you in a week, and that's occasion enough."

He kissed my neck as I set the flowers on the kitchen table.

"Second, we have been *not hating* each other for seven months."

"Not hating?"

He nodded, and his snarky grin grew. "Remember, you hated me at first. I'm counting that day as our first meeting; so, we weren't together, we were *not hating* each other for all that time."

I rolled my eyes and snorted. "You are impossible, Nick Dunlap."

His reply was to grab me about the waist and pull me in for another passionate kiss.

That morning, we proved the Clippers weren't the only team who could play twice in a day. Nick even traded offense for defense in the second round.

As we lay in bed, one messy, sweaty, tangled wreck of exhausted man-flesh, Nick turned on his side and ran his fingers through my hair. His gaze was so intense, so pure, I could barely hold it.

"Everything okay?" I asked.

He smiled, and his hand paused its stroking. "I love you more than anyone or anything in this world. I didn't even know what loving someone felt like until I met you. Now, I can't imagine a day without this feeling, without touching you, feeling you beside me, being part of your life."

He drew in a breath and held it as unspoken thoughts played in his eyes.

"I'm scared, André."

That caught me by surprise. I propped myself up on an elbow and faced him.

"Of what?"

He looked away, then back to me, and his brow furrowed.

"I'm not worried about the season. We'll have travel, and that will suck, but most of the time I'll be here. I'll have plenty of time to visit, to see you and Ethan."

"Okay, so what *does* worry you?"

"What if ... what if I get called up?"

I cocked my head. "I do not understand."

"My stats are strong. The team likes me. I'm good at the PR stuff. What if the franchise pulls me into the majors?"

"Isn't that what you've been working for your whole life? Wouldn't that be wonderful?"

He nodded. "Yeah, of course. The dream of wearing a major league uniform kept me going when my dad ... when everything was so ... It's all I've ever wanted."

He trailed a finger down my cheek.

"All I ever wanted before ... before I met you."

A painful silenced blanketed the bed.

"There isn't a major league team in Columbus. We're an affiliate of Cleveland." His voice trembled.

"Nick, we will deal with that when the day comes. I will be proud of you, will support you, will do everything to help you succeed." I cupped his cheek, and he leaned into my touch. "And yes, we will have to figure things out, but we *will* find a way."

"You really think so?"

His voice sounded so small, so unsure, and a trickle of tears fell to his cheeks.

"I have never loved anyone like I love you. There is nothing in this world strong enough to keep us apart."

He leaned over and pressed his head into my shoulder, and I held him until his tears dried.

Thirty

Nick

Opening day for most teams involved playing a rival, or at least a team who would draw the interest of fans—and get butts in seats. The Clippers chose a very different route, and managed to fill the stadium beyond capacity.

The Memphis Mangoes weren't technically a minor league team. They belonged to a special league of their own (not a "crying in baseball" reference), where the sport was as much about having fun, sharing laughs, and general hilarity as it was the actual game played. The guys on the team were skilled and remarkably athletic. They had to be to perform some of their stunts, but none of them had the skills to make it into the majors. The pressures of the profession were very different in their organization.

The advantage to playing the Mangoes for our season opener was clear: it was an exhibition game that only counted for gate fees and promotional value. The win or loss wouldn't matter because they weren't in our division. They weren't even in our league. It was a beautiful night to play some ball and remember how fun the game could be.

I also looked forward to seeing my old teammate, Nate Stringer, as he took the field in his first year with the Mangoes. Nate had been one of my few friends on the Nashville Sounds, one of the good guys who treated me like a brother despite being an openly gay player. He'd never come out or even expressed an interest in guys, but his close friends were a pack of gays who came to many of our games, leaving me to wonder whether Nate and I might've had more in common than I'd known.

André waved from the front row, right along the first base line, as I emerged from the dugout and trotted onto the field. My heart filled as I caught a glimpse of spindly arms waving wildly beside him and heard Ethan screaming my name as loudly as his little lungs would allow. On his tiny traitorous head was a giant foam mango, but the glove I'd given him waved on his right hand. André had promised to try to bring him, but said he doubted Dr. Marber would allow the impromptu field trip. My man was convincing when he really wanted something.

We finished our warm-up, stood in line for the anthem, then took the field.

As the first Mango stepped up to the plate, I slapped my glove and readied myself.

Then the rest of the Mangoes poured out of their dugout, formed a semi-circle behind the umpire, and began dancing as 'YMCA' blared over the speakers. The crowd leapt to their feet, and thousands of voices joined in the popular tune. Even the ump got in on the act, shaking his enormous butt and making letters with his arms.

Our poor pitcher barely knew what to do.

He walked that first batter, never getting the ball near the plate.

The Mangoes started a chant of, "Whoomp, there it is," as the batter boogied his way to first base. In that moment, every Clipper realized the tone for the night had been set. We were merely pawns in their game, and we might as well just enjoy it.

Nate smacked a double in his first at-bat, early in the second inning. Standing on base, he turned toward me at center and waved.

"Hey, Nick!" he yelled over the roars of the crowd, waving both hands wildly, as if beckoning a plane to the ground with glow sticks.

I laughed and waved back.

Anywhere else, against any other team, it would have been taboo to even acknowledge the gesture. Some umpires would warn or toss a player for that kind of interaction—but playing against the Mangoes, all bets were off. The night was so nutty, I was surprised the boys in the booth hadn't played a voiceover from an old *I Love Lucy* argument to narrate our exchange for the crowd.

In the fourth inning, as our batter readied in the box, the Mangoes' second baseman ran forward, leapfrogged over the pitcher as he bent to tie a shoe, and pitched a perfect strike. Our guy popped a foul high above the first base line, and the darn second baseman darted over and caught it. It was the quirkiest, funniest, most athletic play I'd ever seen.

The crowd erupted. Even our guys applauded and cheered. Then the blaring trumpets of John Williams's 'Olympic Fanfare and Theme' sang over the speakers as all the Mangoes mobbed the player holding his glove aloft, like he'd just caught the final ball of the World Series.

Then I realized who that second baseman was.

Nate Stringer.

You go, old friend. That was awesome.

The game ended with the Mangoes on top 7–4.

No one cared.

The crowd cheered and laughed as the teams came together and shook hands. When Nate reached me, he surprised me with a hug, then pulled back, still gripping my shoulders.

"Meet me in the tunnel after you change. I'd love to catch up. Oh, I have some friends I want you to meet too."

I smacked his arm. "You bet. Looking forward to it. I might have a couple guys of my own for you to meet."

His eyes widened along with his smile, then we were on to shake the next hand.

The stands were always packed with kids when the Mangoes played. Their visits had become one of the favored events of the year for children and parents alike. As such, the Clippers smartly advanced the starting hour of those games to allow moms, dads, and little ones to return home for a reasonable bedtime.

As I strode down the tunnel, headed toward the parking lot, I saw André first, his graying hair swept under a white-and-blue Clippers cap that looked freshly purchased. I barely had time to glance down before Ethan tore himself from André's grasp and barreled into me.

"Nick! That was so awesome. Did you see that guy jump over the pitcher and then throw a strike and then catch it? And Krash raced a giant mango! I've never seen a mango run before. I've never even had a mango."

Krash was the mascot of the Clippers, a green condor wearing a blue-and-gray-striped Clippers jersey.

"Yeah, I saw the crazy pitcher guy," I said, picking him up and tossing him as high as the tunnel's ceiling would allow. The giggles that flowed out of him filled my heart.

As I set him down, I leaned over and whispered, "You want to meet him?"

His eyes became saucers. "No way!"

"Yes way. Turn around."

As slowly as he'd ever moved, Ethan turned around to find Nate standing behind André, now dressed in jeans and a Mangoes t-shirt. He waved and smiled as Ethan met his gaze.

I thought the boy might pass out right there.

"Holy shit!"

"Ethan!" André and I said in unison, then looked at each other and broke out in laughter.

"Hi, little man. I'm Nate. What's your name?"

Ethan gaped. He pointed at Nate, then looked back at me. "That's ... he's ... a real Mango."

I shook my head. "Yes, he is. Tell him your name, goober."

"I'm not a goober!" Then he remembered his new hero and turned. "I'm Ethan. You're awesome."

Nate beamed. "No, you're awesome. That's a really cool glove."

Ethan held his glove up, then turned. "Nick got it for me. I'm his fielding coach."

Nate glanced from Ethan to André to me, then cocked a brow. "I see we *do* have catching up to do."

I noticed several people standing behind Nate and nodded toward them with a questioning gaze.

"Oh, sorry," he said, stepping aside. "This is my much better half, Cooper."

A fit guy with brackish hair tinted with auburn grinned and waved like we stood a field apart.

"And this," he said, motioning past Cooper, "is Sam and Miguel. Watch out for Miguel. He's a cop."

A handsome man with tight-cropped black hair stepped forward, his teeth lighting up the tunnel as they spread nearly from ear to ear. "Don't listen to that grease monkey. Cops are cool."

"Can I see your badge?" Ethan chimed.

"You bet, once we get to dinner, okay?" Miguel said.

Sam, a rugged guy with blue eyes almost as piercing as the White Walkers from *Game of Thrones*, stepped forward and stuck out a meaty hand. "Nice to see you again, Nick. We met back in Nashville once, at the park."

I nodded, wanting him to feel remembered, though I couldn't place ever seeing him before. I would've remembered those eyes.

"Good to see you again, Sam," I said, then glanced around. "How do we feel about a brewpub?"

"Sounds great," Sam said, as Miguel nodded. André didn't look thrilled, but held his tongue. Cooper nodded like a golden retriever who'd just received praise.

The post-game crowd had thinned by the time we arrived at the restaurant, so we were quickly ushered to a round eight-top.

"So," Nate sat next to me and leaned over. "You, André, *and* Ethan?"

I grinned. "Ethan's one of the kids at the place where André works. He's a great kid. I've been kind of doing the big brother thing. André is ... well, he's serious."

"Oh?"

"Like, he's *the one*, serious."

He whistled. "That was fast. Didn't you just get here six months ago?"

"Seven, thank you very much, and it did kind of happen fast." I glanced past him at Cooper. "All that time on the same team and I didn't even know you were gay. He's dreamy."

Nate beamed. "Yeah, he is, and he's smarter than both of us combined."

I grunted. "Wait until you get to know André. I feel smarter just sitting next to him, like it rubs off or something."

He chuckled, then eyed Ethan. "You sure you're just that little guy's big brother? Sure looked like—"

"It's a long story. He's a special kid."

"Are you two colluding?" André's voice broke our huddle.

"Why? Your ears burning?" I teased.

"With you? Always. Nate, do not believe this one. He is sneaky."

Nate grinned. "You don't know me, André. I'm far worse."

Cooper, who none of us realized had been paying attention, leaned across Nate and said, "He's not lying. He's the sneakiest one of the bunch, unless you count me because no one thinks I would ever sneak at all but that's exactly when I sneak up on them and that's funny because everyone jumps and screams, except Sam over there, he squeals, and for such a rugged guy, that's even funnier than when other people yell."

None of us knew what to say to that.

It was like the room's oxygen had been completely exhausted by Cooper's Charles Dickens declaration.

"You're funny," Ethan said, summarizing everything I was thinking and completely shattering the moment.

Dinner devolved into one overlapping conversation after another. Nate and André ganged up on me, while Sam and Miguel teased Cooper relentlessly. For some reason, Cooper kept referring to the pair as "Mom and Dad," the last nicknames I would've expected of the pair, but they wore the monikers with pride. Ethan, struggling to decide whether he wanted to be a cop or a Mango when he grew up, peppered Miguel and Nate with question after question.

The whole thing felt more like a family reunion than a post-game dinner with a fellow player and fans.

When the check arrived and each of us stood, Nate gripped my shoulder. "It's good to see you happy, Nick. I hated how things went down in Nashville. The team lost a great player when you left."

"Thanks, Nate." Something caught in my throat at the sincerity in his eyes. André's hand found my other shoulder, and I leaned back into the comfort of his chest. "Everything worked out for the best."

"I see that," Nate said, smiling. He hesitated a moment, then pulled Cooper into our circle. "Coop and I are planning something, and we'd like to invite the two of you, if you don't mind coming to Tennessee for a few days."

"Okay, we're listening," I said.

"We're getting married," Coop blurted. "He asked me to be his Mango, and I said yes."

It took a second to register, as I was learning it usually did when Cooper opened his mouth, then André and I lunged forward to hug the happy couple.

"Of course, we'll come down if I can get away from the team," I said.

"We're thinking next off-season. A lot of the people we care about have the same problem," Nate said.

"That'll work. Congratulations, Nate! I really am happy for you," I whispered in Nate's ear, unsure why we were sharing such an intimate moment. I didn't know him well. We hadn't been close on the Sounds, but the moment we reunited, it felt like the brother I'd never had showed up.

"Thanks, brother," he whispered back, sealing our familial pact.

Nate and Cooper drove away, leaving Sam and Miguel at Ethan's mercy. He now bounced between the cool cars Sam worked on as a mechanic, and how he might want to grow up to work in a garage, to losing his little mind when Miguel flashed his badge.

"Do you have a gun? Can I see it?"

"Oh no, little man. No guns for you," I said, mussing his hair.

Sam eyed me and grinned.

"What?"

"Motherhood suits you."

André snorted.

"If there wasn't a kid present, I tell you—"

"To frog off," Ethan finished my sentence, sort of.

We all burst out laughing.

"Frog off?" I asked Ethan.

He nodded seriously. "Yeah. That's what adults say when they're mad. Frog you. Frog off. You know. I don't get why frogs mean you're mad, but they do."

Miguel was practically wheezing. He turned to Sam. "Babe, we need to frog off now. I can't take any more."

"Frog you. Get in the car," Sam replied.

"You two are froggin' impossible," I said, then turned to André.

He covered my mouth with his palm before I could speak.

His words were clipped and precise. "Do not dare call this Frenchman a frog."

Miguel's laughter lingered long after they drove away.

Thirty-One

André

Weeks of baseball quickly turned into months. The Clippers entered the summer months with a winning record, and Nick led the league with a batting average he swore couldn't last. He'd gone from a discarded player to one of the team's most respected leaders.

In the first three months of Nick's time in blue, his coach only called one two-a-day, which meant, when they played in town, he brought me lunch and played ball with Ethan. Some days, he even helped with the boy's homework. Their bond had only grown stronger, despite Nick's stints on the road.

Zack and Kervin were ever-present. It didn't matter what we planned, that pair found their way into the center of it. Marcus joined us for dinner at least once each week, and I made a point to attend as many games as possible. I had never been part of a close-knit group of friends, but it only took a few months for those guys to become an integral part of our world. Ethan even took to calling Marcus "Uncle *Papai*." Nick had taught him *papi*, but Marcus corrected him, offering the Portuguese term instead.

The big man was Jell-O around Ethan. We all were.

On June 12, Nick and I were munching on sandwiches in my office when his phone rang. I remember the date because I saw it below his agent's name on his phone. My heart leapt into my throat as he answered.

He barely spoke after the initial greeting. When he set his phone on the table, his face was an unreadable mask.

"Well? You cannot leave me in suspense," I said, unable to wait for him to speak.

"I got the call." His voice was a whisper bathed in a rasp. "André, I ... I got the call. I can't believe it's real." He looked up; tears brimmed in his eyes. "I'm a major league player."

I dove around the table and wrapped him in my arms. "I am so proud of you, Nick. You deserve this so much."

He pulled back, his eyes still staring without seeing. "They're giving me a million-dollar salary. A *million* dollars."

My breath caught. "Jesus. I knew they paid a lot of money, but that's—"

"A frogging lot of money."

"We need to celebrate. When do you go? Where are you going? I know so little about how this works."

His face fell.

"What? Nick, what is it?"

"I'm playing for Cleveland, like we thought." His eyes met mine. "I report in two days."

"Two *days*?" I sat back onto the floor.

He nodded. "How far away is Cleveland?"

"A little over two hours, maybe more with traffic. A flight barely takes off before it lands."

"That's not too bad," he said, without conviction.

"Nick, listen to me." I took his hands. "This is wonderful news! You have worked for this your whole life. Everything about this is happy, amazing, and unbelievable. It is a dream come true."

"But—"

"No but. You do not get a but tonight."

A grin flashed briefly in his eyes.

"Okay, you may have a butt with two Ts, not the kind with one T."

"I like your butt," he muttered.

"It likes you too, but we're talking about celebrating. We need to call the guys."

"They have a game tonight, but tomorrow's an off day for the team."

"Perfect. We can go without worrying about staying out too late." I patted his leg.

His eyes dropped to my hand. "I need to spend the afternoon with Ethan. How am I supposed to tell him I'm leaving?"

"He will miss you. We all will, but you have to live your dream. You have to teach him how to live a dream, that they *can* come true if you work hard enough. He deserves that lesson, from you."

Nick looked up. "How'd you get so smart?"

I grinned. "Finally, as you're leaving, you realize I'm smart? *Mon dieu!*"

The franchise sent people to pack Nick's apartment, which took all of an hour, so we had the entire day to enjoy together. I took a much-needed vacation day, and Dr. Marber let us take Ethan to the zoo.

Watching Nick watch Ethan as he witnessed the wonders of nature for the first time was adorable. Ethan couldn't decide which exhibit had been his favorite: the elephants for their "awesome strength," the monkeys for their agility, or the seals, because they reminded him of playful, swimming dogs, with their cute expressions and silly antics.

We ate terrible fried food covered in powdered sugar, like attendees at some rustic annual fair. Despite his age, Ethan was still small enough for Nick to cart around on his shoulders, something the boy said he'd never experienced. As we stood before one exhibit, two of the young mandrills, the monkeys with fuzzy hair and a long, striped snout, decided to mirror the funny humans, one attempting to climb on the other's shoulders. The little guy lost his balance before gaining his perch and tumbled back into a pile of wood chips.

Ethan's incessant giggles drew smiles from everyone we passed.

By the time we left the animal sanctuary mid-afternoon, my heart was full.

And heavy.

Nick and Ethan said a tearful goodbye as we dropped him back at the Ranch. The boy clung to him, sobbing and begging for him to stay. As much as I knew this was the right move for Nick, I wanted to join in wrapping my arms around him and pleading for more time together. The three of us wept until Sara arrived to take Ethan from Nick one last time.

"God, that was awful," he said as we sat in the car, staring blankly at the building where Ethan lived.

I reached across and took his hand. "You gave him a wonderful day, Nick, and so much more than that. He is a beautiful, happy little boy again—because of you. Focus on that."

"I love him, André. I love him so much." He began to sob. "It feels like my heart is tearing apart. Hearing him cry ... oh god ..."

I wrapped him in my arms and struggled to keep my own tears at bay. I wanted to let it all out, to scream and cry, to grab onto Nick and not let go. I wanted to rage at a world so beautiful it had given me love again, then stolen it away. I wanted to be angry and hurt. I wanted to curl into a ball and shut the world out until the clouds parted.

But I had to be strong for him—for *both* of them.

"I know. He loves you too."

We left one farewell to attend the next.

What began as Marcus, Zack, and Kervin taking us to dinner following a home game evolved into the entire Clippers organization hosting a celebration in honor of one of their own. Every player, coach, manager, front office person—even a couple of the grounds crew—showed up at Taft's.

Over the course of the season, I'd met most of the players, and was pleasantly surprised at how accepting, even caring, the guys were toward each other—and toward me. It was truly a baseball family, special and unique.

Coach Garzon rose, and everyone quieted.

"I don't need to tell you why we're here. Fuckin' Dunlap couldn't even stick around for a full season."

A roar of laughter and jeers swelled.

"I'm not sure how he did it, but if that dumbass can hit .408 through half the season, the rest of you can get above the Mendoza Line."

Another swell, this time more grumble than assent. Coach had hit a nerve with a few of the players struggling at the plate.

"Enough of me. We're here for Nick. Get up here and say goodbye to your brothers."

Nick's eyes bulged. He hadn't planned to speak to the group. He hadn't known there would even be a group.

"Coach, I'm good—"

A thunderous chant of "Dun-lap, Dun-lap, Dun-lap" brought him to his feet.

"Alright," he said, waving his arms for them to kill the chant. "I'll try."

It took a second for the team to settle, as a few wanted nothing more than to give Nick grief while he struggled with his emotions—boys being boys, and all.

"I'm really pumped about playing at the next level. I mean, who here wouldn't be? It's the dream of every minor leaguer." The guys nodded. "But I gotta say, today's been tough."

The room became eerily quiet.

A server somewhere across the restaurant clanked a plate.

One of the players set his beer down hard on the wooden tabletop.

"I said goodbye to ..." Nick sucked in a breath. "Now I have to do it again, to all of you."

I lost my battle, and tears began streaming down my cheeks.

"After Nashville, I mean, you guys know how that went down, I didn't know what to expect up here. Kervin, Zack, Marcus—all of you guys—you took me in, treated me like I'd always been here, like I was just one of the guys."

"You are, asshole," Tex called out from the back, earning a round of chuckles.

"Thanks, Tex. Love you too." That won a few more laughs. "Anyway, I just want to say thanks. And, if I can make it to the bigs, anybody here can."

"Damn right," Marcus shouted, his voice snapping Nick's head in his direction long enough for the two to exchange nods.

"Like Coach said, I've only been here half a season, but it feels like a lot longer. You guys are awesome, and, well, I guess I'm gonna miss you."

"You guess?" one player called out.

"You still here, asshole?" another shouted.

The place erupted in playful banter and heartfelt laughter. Any sentimental mood was shattered, and Nick escaped without a single tear shed. I grabbed a wad of napkins and dried mine before he could notice.

That night, as we lay in bed together for the last time as a non-long-distance couple, unbidden tears returned. My universe was unraveling, and my heart felt like someone was pounding it with a mallet. Breathing had become a desperate battle.

But I had to be strong.

He tried to ease the pain I'd failed miserably to hide. "I'll come home as much as I can. We're just two hours away. And you can come up anytime. I don't know my schedule yet, but we'll plan it all out, okay?"

I nodded and cupped his cheek, desperate to imprint his warmth on my heart and mind.

"And Ethan, do you think they'll let you bring him to games in Cleveland?"

"Oh, Nick. I don't know about that. A day trip to the zoo was one thing, but to travel outside the city ... I don't think Dr. Marber would accept that."

His eyes fell, and I cringed as waves of grief wafted off him.

When our eyes met—his overflowing—I gave a pathetic answer, the only promise I knew I could keep. My heart knew better than to offer more hope than two fragile words: "I'll try."

We didn't make love that night. Sex seemed so small next to what we faced. The idea of it felt like making our goodbye more real, more permanent. I wanted nothing to do with permanence—unless it included Nick.

Enjoying the comfort of each other's arms was more than enough.

It was what I knew I would miss the most.

Thirty-Two

Nⁱᶜᵏ

T he first week with the Guardians was nuts. Between press events with local media, interviews with major cable networks, and finding my way around another new city, I was nearly overwhelmed.

Then I walked into my new home, Progressive Field.

The tunnel was wide, its floor perfectly polished. The locker room included comfy, well-worn leather couches, TVs on nearly every wall, and enough space for a team twice our size to change without bumping into each other.

I slowly walked around the banks of lockers, staring at the names etched in golden plaques above each bay. These were my heroes, guys who'd made it to the mountaintop and paved the way for others, like me, to join them. I could barely believe it when I reached the shiny new plaque bearing my name. I ran a finger over it, feeling each curve and indention, not trusting my eyes that it was real.

A jersey hung below. I flipped it around and smiled at "Dunlap" stitched across the back above the number twenty-seven, the same digits I'd worn since the first days on my high school team.

"This is real. I made it," I muttered.

"Every guy who walks in here does what you're doing. Seen it a hundred times, probably more."

I spun to find a man, stooped with age and topped with snow, smiling warmly in my direction as he leaned on a dry mop. His bushy brows looked like they might take flight at any moment.

"Uh, hey. I'm Nick."

He snorted. "Yeah, I know who you are. Welcome to the team."

"Thanks. I'm sorry, I didn't get your name," I said.

His smile widened. "Good man. A lot of the guys don't bother asking, think it's beneath them now or something. Name's Max, but everybody's called me Scooter since my days on the team."

"You played ball?"

He chuckled. "Look me up, kid. Max LeMerc. Add 1968 to make Google happy. Good luck. I'll be pulling for ya."

"Thanks, Max—uh, Scooter," I said, waving like a dumbass as he shuffled out of the locker room.

On impulse, I grabbed my phone and plugged in his name.

"Holy shit."

The janitor had played for ten years at the major league level, even won his own World Series ring. What in the world was he doing mopping our floors?

I tossed that, and the other dozen questions racing through my mind, into my mental locker and stepped to a set of double doors. I could hear staff going through their gameday preparations outside, but still hesitated. There would never be another "first time." I wanted to savor this moment, to etch it in my memory.

I pulled the doors open and strode into a wall of summer heat. The dugout was clean, with bats in their bins, coolers filled with iced drinks, and batting helmets polished and gleaming in the sunlight. The smell of cut grass filled my lungs, and I welcomed it into my soul. I took the three steps to place a foot on the red clay and smiled as my impression remained.

I had already left a mark.

Then I laughed out loud at the silliness of my musing. I was a major league baseball player. My job was to catch and smack balls, not create poetry out of dirt and air.

Still, as I reached the grass, I knelt and ran my fingers through it. I couldn't help myself. The little kid who'd dreamed of this day was screaming in my chest, dancing with all the joy and exuberance of untainted youth.

I'd really done it. I still couldn't believe it was true.

"You're Dunlap, right?" a youthful voice called from beyond first base.

I snapped up to find a guy in a practice uniform trotting toward me. I held up a hand to shield my eyes. "Yeah, I'm Nick."

"For now," the player grunted. "Once Van gets hold of you, you'll have a new name." He grinned as he reached me and stuck out a hand. "I'm Parker Hughes. Play second."

I giggled like a child. "Batted .305 last season. One error. Almost won a Golden Glove."

He nodded, and his grin widened. "Still a fan? We'll fix that in time."

"Nah. This'll never get old. You're awesome, man. Really. I'm just happy to be here."

"Bullshit," he said, a verbal punch to the gut. "You're a fucking Guardian now. You deserve the jersey. Play like it. Act like it. Never doubt it."

I stared a second, then nodded. "Thanks."

"Don't thank me. Prove me right." Then he swatted my shoulder with his glove. "Get geared up. You can warm me up, let me see what you've got."

Thirty-Three

ANDRÉ

The summer was hot and incredibly busy at the Ranch. We treated children, youth, and entire families; the pandemic had caused a surge of need that had yet to fully work its way through our community. In addition to our more permanent residents, hundreds flowed through our doors seeing counseling, healing, and restored hope.

I spent as much time with Ethan as I could. He played with his peers, participated fully in his sessions, and was generally the happy boy I'd come to love, but the spark in his eyes that warmed my heart had dimmed with Nick's absence. There wasn't a single time we spent together that he didn't ask about his adopted big brother. He watched as many of his games as he could catch on television, and had memorized most of his stats. For a child his age, he had an impressive memory.

Nick had found a beautiful house on a sprawling pasture with a small pond just outside of town. I knew he had to settle into his new life, but the act of buying a home in Cleveland felt like another nail in the coffin of our time together in Columbus. My rational mind scolded my heart for being jealous, but I was. I was jealous of Cleveland, of his team, of baseball, of everything that was standing between Nick living with me, building a life with me.

But jealousy has never been a worthy friend.

Nick kept his promise, visiting as often as he could, which turned out to be once every couple weeks. His team rarely had more than one day off at a time, so our visits were brief, but even those short respites offered Ethan and me the boost we needed to make it until our next reunion.

Dr. Marber, as expected, rejected my request to take Ethan to Cleveland. It was simply beyond the bounds of the Ranch's appetite for legal liability. I couldn't blame her. It was a hard request to make, and one I would likely have turned down had the decision landed on my desk.

The all-star break was an unexpected blessing. Nick had four days off. There were no practices, no games, no press events, nothing. He couldn't drive home fast enough, stepping into my house just after four o'clock. I couldn't hold him close enough, feel him deep enough, kiss him long enough. We stripped each other naked and didn't put on clothes again until noon the next day.

While Dr. Marber had refused our request to take Ethan out of the city, she surprised us by allowing him to stay at my home throughout the rest of the visit. On our first day, we visited Nick's old ballpark so Ethan could meet the team. Marcus insisted on playing catch, sending our little chatterbox into a world-class tizzy. Nick and I watched, and I wasn't sure which of those boys we stared at more. Marcus truly was a work of art.

That night, after a fun-filled day, Ethan passed out with his head in Nick's lap as we watched *Survivor*. I smoothed the hair off his forehead and savored the rise and fall of his little chest. Nick pressed a kiss to his head, sending my heart to the moon. When Tribal Council ended and a player was sent packing, Nick lifted the limp lad and carried him into the bedroom, where he slept soundly between us. That night, we endured bony elbows and knobby knees digging into our ribs.

The next morning, I was the first to wake. I rubbed my eyes and yawned, debating a mental snooze versus starting the day. Then I glanced at my boys. Ethan's head rested on Nick's chest, while Nick's arm held him snugly in place. I'd never imagined a more peaceful, more beautiful sight.

The rest of that week passed far too quickly, heralding Nick's return to Cleveland and Ethan's return to the Ranch. I dreaded kissing Nick goodbye again. What I hadn't expected was how hard it was to return

Ethan to the care of my peers. I watched him walk through the lobby, pause at the double doors, then turn and wave back at me—and my heart seized.

Why? Why should it bother me to bring him back? Am I just overly emotional because Nick left?

That must be it. That's all this is.

I was a professional. I worked with children all day. Hell, I worked with Ethan. He wasn't flying to some distant land. I would see him again in a few hours.

He was only a building away.

And yet, it felt as though a part of me had walked through those double doors.

A part of me had waved goodbye.

Thirty-Four

Nick

I didn't know it was possible for time to both fly and drag, but the second half of the season felt exactly like that. Games came and went, and before I knew it, September—and the regular season—was nearly done, and the Guardians were headed into the playoffs.

I was both thrilled at my new team's performance, and frustrated that André and I had to wait another month to be together.

Time was a fickle mistress.

But humility had a wicked sense of humor.

The interstellar batting average I'd enjoyed as a Clipper was brought to earth by the pitching skills of superhuman athletes glaring down from the mound, completely unperturbed by the rookie staring back at them. I quickly learned just how large the leap was from the minors to the majors, especially the expertise of the pitching staffs.

Still, my performance at the plate was solid, while my defensive game was exceptional. There was even talk among the press of me being considered for Rookie of the Year. I was still numb from getting to play major league ball, of wearing a jersey and playing in a stadium with tens of thousands of fans. Awards were beyond my brain's ability to compute.

All the while, my semimonthly trips to Columbus felt further and further apart, never coming fast enough or lasting long enough, each offering welcome relief yet tearing at my heart with every parting.

We celebrated our one-year not-hating-each-other-versary over FaceTime.

How do military families live like this? I wondered, as I drove back one Thursday. *They go months or years without each other. It must be awful.*

On the third of October, as a stiff breeze drifted across the grass, I jogged onto the field in my first major league post-season game. The stadium was overflowing with rowdy, obnoxiously loud, fervently devoted fans who lived for the game and clung desperately to the dream of another World Series win.

Back at the Ranch, André sat in the middle of Marcus, Kervin, and Zack, while Ethan was wedged in the midst of a pack of squirming children. Everyone staring at the large screen TV in the common room.

We faced the Tampa Bay Rays—in Tampa.

We'd had a good season. They'd been otherworldly.

Our regular season ended with ninety-two wins and seventy losses, for a division-leading average of nearly fifty-seven percent. Theirs was nearly seventy percent, putting them near the top of the major league's all-time team-winning percentage charts with the likes of the 1906 Chicago Cubs and the 1909 Pittsburgh Pirates.

Still, the state of Ohio—and, especially, a certain common room—vibrated with hope.

We lost game one 11–2.

In game two, our defense committed a season-high five errors, and we handed the Rays a 14–3 victory.

The next game was played at home at Progressive Field. André and the guys drove up and cheered from the players' section midway up the first base line.

Game three wasn't as close as the first two, and our season came to an abrupt end before the first week of October had the good grace to pass.

"Dude, that was one hell of a season," Zack said, grabbing my outstretched palm and pulling me into a hug. Kervin made it a group hug, adding, "You've had a great year, man, making it into the majors and playing like a king. You should be proud."

I smiled weakly. After a three-game, ass-kicking sweep, it was hard to feel pride.

Marcus loomed over me, his meaty paws nearly encircling my arms. "Roomie, you were the shit. I am Brazilian. I know my shit."

I wasn't totally sure what he meant, but took his laughter as a good sign and gave him a friendly nod.

Then André stepped up, and I fell into his arms.

"I am so proud of you, Nick. You showed our children how to live their dreams. You should have seen them gathered around the television, watching *their* Nick."

"God, I miss Ethan."

André refused to let go. "It wasn't just Ethan. All of the children were there. They believe in you. They believe in *themselves* a little more *because of you*."

We pulled apart, and I found such depth in his eyes.

"I ... André, thank you. I can't wait to get home."

"Listen, you two," Kervin interjected, killing the moment. "If we don't feed Marcus soon, bad things will happen."

Marcus agreed. "Yes, I will have to eat out Kervin."

An astonished moment later, pandemonium erupted as the meaning of Marcus's shattered English sank in.

"Hey! He was *my* roommate. If anyone gets eaten out by the big lug, it's me."

Zack doubled over, Kervin was in tears, and poor Marcus towered above us all, bouncing from one laughing friend to the next, utterly clueless at what he'd said.

There was no need for me to rent an apartment. I moved from my place in Cleveland into André's house. We replaced André's small dresser and a few other pieces to give my things a rightful place. Gone were the days of me occupying a drawer or two. We were together, our lives commingled, in every way that mattered.

I wanted it to feel like coming home, but something in me knew it would never be so again—neither André's house, nor Columbus.

By the time our second Thanksgiving together arrived, life had returned to a beautiful rhythm. Most of my days were spent working out and spending time with Ethan. He'd turned nine that year, yet another milestone I'd missed while on a road trip. He changed every day, grew taller and sharper, opened himself up a tiny bit more. It was remarkable to watch, like seeing a flower open in one of those sped-up nature specials.

I hadn't thought it was possible to crave seeing the little guy more than before, but now that I was back, there was nowhere I'd rather have been than with him and André.

In the first week of December, as André and I sat at his table sipping our morning coffee, my phone rang.

"Why would your agent be calling?"

My heart began to race. "No clue."

As it turned out, there was a sponsorship opportunity with a local car dealership, and my agent wanted permission to pitch me. It should've been a positive call, something worth celebrating. Sponsorships meant more money with reasonably little time commitment. They were one of the primary business goals of every professional athlete.

So, why did the call feel like a gut-punch?

André's face was ashen. My stomach ached.

I couldn't take this anymore.

"Babe, we have to do something. We were only apart for half a season. I can't stand the thought of being without you for eight months."

He nodded slowly. "I have given this a great deal of thought."

I waited. He sat frozen.

"And?"

"I could not find a solution, Nick. I do not know what to do."

I dropped to my knees before him. "I do, André. Come to Cleveland. There has to be a place like the Ranch in Cleveland, maybe at the Cleveland Clinic? We'll find you somewhere you'll love to work, somewhere with kids who need a wonderful, crazy Frenchman to help them."

He wagged a finger. "I am not crazy, merely French."

"Yes, my dear, you are both crazy *and* French, but I love you anyway." I grinned with a confidence I didn't feel, then grabbed his hands and pulled him toward me. "Marry me, André. Marry me and move to Cleveland. Let's start a new life together. I already have more house than I can stand. Hell, a cardboard box would feel empty without you."

"You want to put me into a cardboard box?"

"Listen, you," I growled. "This isn't how I wanted to propose—or how I ever dreamed of it—but I can't wait any longer. We'll do this right later, just say yes to me now. Say yes to *us*."

"You are asking me to leave the Ranch?"

"If I could do my job anywhere, I would, but you know I can't. Please, babe, say yes."

His chair creaked.

A tree limb battered his kitchen window.

My heart thudded against my chest.

"*Oui.*"

"*Oui* what?"

"*Oui* to everything, Nick Dunlap. *Oui*, I will marry you. *Oui*, I will quit my job and sell my house. *Oui*, I will move to the ends of the earth to be with you. You are everything to me, Nick. Everything."

I rose from my knees and lifted him to his feet, then pressed my lips into his and hugged him with all my strength. It felt like the world had tipped over, and I was falling off the edge, like a herd of wild beasts were rampaging through my chest—like my life had just begun.

And then my brain, the traitorous bastard, spoke through my mouth.

"What about Ethan?"

André smiled and cupped my cheek.

"I have thought a great deal about him too."

Thirty–Five

Nick

C hristmas had never been a particularly important holiday to me. We weren't a religious household, and, after my mom died, my dad barely acknowledged birthdays or holidays.

André and I were determined to make holidays special.

Blinking lights crawled up trees and across the eaves of his house. His yard was decked with prancing deer, a blow-up Santa, and several miniature Guardian mascots dressed in elf costumes. Santa had thrown up all over the interior of his home. I'd never seen so much tinsel and garland. The Christmas tree in his den scraped the ceiling and had taken us half a day to fully decorate, mostly because André kept taking things off and repositioning them "to make them more perfect."

The Pentatonix crew sang Christmas music in the background as André juggled boiling pots and steaming pans. I'd started setting the table, laying out our best red-and-green placemats, holly-painted plates, and Rudolf silverware.

Yes, André had silverware with reindeer heads on the handles.

In the midst of this Christmas preparation bliss, a knock startled us out of our tasks.

"I've got it," I said, giving him a kiss on the neck.

He had stopped stirring and was staring at the door like it was a leopard about to pounce.

"Dr. Marber, it's great to see you again," I said, letting the Ranch's fearless leader into our home. Ethan stood behind her, and threw himself into my arms the moment she entered.

"Merry Christmas, Nick."

I buried my face in his neck for a zerbert.

He giggled and squirmed.

When I let him down, his eyes widened as he scanned the room, seeing the wonderland we'd created for his arrival.

"Whoa! This is so cool," he said, his voice filled with awe.

Dr. Marber smiled, and I think that was the first time I'd ever seen her do that.

It was a little creepy. She really needed to stop.

"André, thank you for having me over for lunch," she said, turning toward my fiancé. "I won't be able to stay long as I still have to cook for my clan in a couple hours."

"Of course. Thank you for joining us, and for bringing Ethan."

André turned to Ethan. "Would you like to stay here this weekend? Enjoy Christmas with Nick and me?"

"Can I?" he asked Dr. Marber. "Please?"

She laughed and patted his head, like he was some dog she'd just fostered. "It's why you're here, silly. Of course you can."

"Lunch is almost ready," André said. "Nick, would you help Ethan get cleaned up?"

"Sure. Come on, little man," I said, grabbing him and tickling his ribs, hearing my favorite giggle in the world.

As we entered the bathroom, I heard Dr. Marber ask, "Are you sure about this, André? This is your home."

I couldn't hear his response over the running water and babbling child.

An hour later, our plates were littered with the remains of beef bourguignon. André had truly outdone himself with a dish that he'd started two days ago. It might've been the best thing I'd ever tasted.

"Well, gentlemen, I must be on my way. But I believe we had a business matter to discuss," Dr. Marber said, primly dabbing the corners of her mouth with her napkin.

"I'll go watch TV," Ethan said, sensing an adult conversation.

I wrapped an arm around his chest and pulled him into me. "I think you should stay."

He shoved away and eyed me. "Why?"

I chuckled. He was such a smart little thing.

"Well, we want to ask you something."

"Okaaaay," he said, the drawn-out A underscoring his growing sense of suspicion.

André stood, walked around behind me, and placed a hand on my shoulder. Ethan's eyes narrowed as they followed him, then darted to Dr. Marber and back to me. He crossed his little arms.

"Ethan, you don't have to answer right now. It's okay if you want to think about this. Just listen to Nick and Dr. Martin, alright?" Dr. Marber said.

Ethan nodded slowly.

"Ethan." I swallowed hard and gripped André's hand on my shoulder. "Ethan, André and I love each other and have decided to get married."

I waited. He didn't budge, didn't blink. His arms remained crossed.

"And, well ... we are moving to Cleveland because that's where my team is. André will be leaving the Ranch soon."

Ethan's eyes began to water, and I realized I'd better make this quick.

"We want to adopt you, Ethan. We want you to come with us, to live with us forever. Will you be our son?"

His face exploded into a blinding flash of teeth and tears, then he leapt into my arms and locked himself around my neck so tight I could barely breathe. André was crying by then, and dropped to his knees to join our hug. I glanced up, through clouded eyes, to find the granite form of Dr. Marber dabbing her eyes as she'd done her mouth not long before.

"You want to be my dad, Nick? Really? Don't lie to me. Please don't."

I completely lost it. "Ethan, I love you, son. I love you so much. I want to be your dad so much it hurts. Please, say yes."

"YES! Yes, yes, yes, yes, yes."

By then, the sobs had taken control and we devolved into a puddle of blubbering boys.

Dr. Marber said something about cooking, then turned and fled, leaving a happy boy and his two overjoyed dads to celebrate their first holiday.

Epilogue

Dear Reader,

 Buckeye isn't your typical MM romance, but as I began typing, my heart knew it was a story that needed telling. This began as a simple tale of two unlikely men, but became so much more when I witnessed Nick fall into a father's love with Ethan. That wasn't planned. Nick did that on his own, and I am so thankful to him for guiding my pen in that direction.

As I said before we began, many of the characters and situations in this book were born of memories of kids who passed through my sister's home over the years. I can still picture her first house with its sprawling yard next to a stand of woods. I see clearly the children who made the shade beneath those trees their world—for a time.

Ethan was real.

We were the same age, but he was a quarter smaller than me—and I was never a giant. He was such a good kid, loving and kind, always with a bright smile and glimmer in his eyes. I remember the day he was adopted, the way he clung to his "forever mom" in my sister's driveway, the way my sister tried to hide her tears, the tears of a foster mom watching yet another child leave her home. They were salty-sweet tears of a woman who loved—and still loves—broader and deeper than any sea.

Noah was real.

Even now, decades later, I can see him in my mind, with his stringy black hair just touching his shoulders and a rebellious set to his jaw. My sister hated that hair, always wanted to cut it. I thought it made him look so cool.

Noah kept to himself, often with his arms crossed and a defiant chin buried in his chest, but for whatever reason, he opened up to me, spent time in my imaginary worlds, became my friend—and I became his.

I remember overhearing my sister and her husband talking about our kinship, marveling that a seventeen-year-old would take a boy of seven or eight (I can't remember) under his wing. They hoped our relationship might be the crack in Noah's armor to allow positive change into his heart, but my mom's alarm bells sounded, and she intervened. I resented it at the time, her stealing me away from my idol.

At the time, I couldn't understand why Noah and I weren't the perfect pair, why my makeshift brother was too ... Noah ... to be my friend.

Today, with the perspective of adulthood and time, her fears make sense. He was seventeen, and I was seven. Her parental apprehension overrode the potential for Noah's progress, however sad that may have been.

For all of Noah's faults and challenges, he was never a danger to me, only to himself. Our friendship was real. His trust and the confessions he shared, only with me, perhaps because I was too young to fully comprehend them, I believe were true.

Noah left the system and my sister's home when he turned eighteen. I hope he made it, made something of himself, but my heart fears more likely outcomes.

In *Buckeye*, I risked the ire of some readers by leaving his story unresolved. I sought to be true to a young man I deeply admired as a child. I don't know what became of him, and fictionalizing a false happy ending felt . . . wrong.

My vision, my memory, is through the clouded eyes of youth. I don't know what might've happened had we remained close. Would he have opened up further, been willing to accept help? Would he have become the influence my mother feared, steering me far from my own path?

I'll never know.

What I do know is that he was deeply troubled, spent time in and out of the juvenile penal system—and he was kind to me. He listened to my incessant babbling, and shared his own. My sister was a new caregiver at the time and was ill-equipped for a challenging older teen like Noah, especially when she had a half-dozen other children at the time. She did her best, but we'll never know if it was enough.

I hope it was.

In the end, I wanted *Buckeye* to be a story of depth and love.

Depth, because the challenges and trials of these children are real and need to be known.

Love, because it is a *verb*, an action, a willing deed. It is more powerful than any challenge or trial, any system or person or ... anything. When given freely, it can heal. When offered without remorse, it can work miracles.

Ethan is all grown up now.

He's still smaller than anyone his age, and still catches an unbearable amount of good-natured shit for it, but he is a giant in my eyes. He and his wife have nine children: three birth, two adopted, and four foster.

My sister's love is a flowering garden that blooms far beyond its walls.

REFERENCE

Buckeye Ranch

The Buckeye Ranch is a real place where amazing people do incredible work. Learn more, donate, or volunteer here.

Chicken Chasseur

A French classic that never seems to go out of style, this dish combines mushrooms and chicken in a tomato and white wine sauce.

Ingredients

- 1 tablespoon cooking oil

- 4 bone-in chicken breasts (about 2¼ pounds in all)

- 1 teaspoon kosher salt, divided

- ½ teaspoon freshly ground black pepper, divided

- 1 tablespoon butter

- 1 onion, chopped

- ¾ pound mushrooms, sliced

- 2 cloves garlic, minced

- 1½ teaspoons flour

- 6 tablespoons dry vermouth or dry white wine

- ⅔ cup canned low-sodium chicken broth or homemade stock

- 1 cup canned crushed tomatoes, drained

- ¼ teaspoon dried thyme

- 2 tablespoons fresh parsley, chopped

Directions

1. In a large, deep frying pan, heat the oil over a moderately high heat. Season the chicken with a quarter-teaspoon each of the salt and pepper and add to the pan. Cook until browned, turning, about 8 minutes in all. Remove. Pour off all but 1 tablespoon of fat from the pan.

2. Add the butter to the pan and reduce the heat to moderately low. Add the onion and cook, stirring occasionally, until translucent, about 5 minutes. Raise the heat to moderately high. Add the mushrooms, garlic, and a quarter-teaspoon of the salt. Cook, stirring frequently, until the vegetables are browned, about 5 minutes.

3. Add the flour and cook, stirring, for 30 seconds. Stir in the vermouth and bring back to a simmer. Stir in the broth, tomatoes, thyme, and the remaining half-teaspoon of salt. Add the chicken and any accumulated juices. Reduce the

heat; simmer, covered, until the chicken is done, about 10 minutes. Stir in the parsley and the remaining quarter-teaspoon of pepper.

Also By Casey

About Your Author

Casey Morales is an LGBT story-teller and the author of multiple international bestselling MM romance novels. Born in the Southern United States, Casey is an avid tennis player, aspiring chef, dog lover, and ravenous consumer of gummy bears. He and his husband, Heath (yes, *that* Heath, from Raised by Wolves), live in Florida.